# THE BREWPUB COOKBOOK

## FAVORITE RECIPES FROM GREAT BREWPUB KITCHENS

# DARIA LABINSKY
# & STAN HIERONYMUS

TIME LIFE®
BOOKS

TIME-LIFE BOOKS, ALEXANDRIA, VIRGINIA
PRINTED IN CANADA.

TIME-LIFE BOOKS IS A DIVISION OF TIME LIFE INC.


TIME-LIFE CUSTOM PUBLISHING

| | |
|---|---|
| Vice President and Publisher | Terry Newell |
| Associate Publisher | Teresa Hartnett |
| Vice President of Sales and Marketing | Neil Levin |
| Project Manager | Jennifer Michelle Lee |
| Director of Special Sales | Liz Ziehl |
| Managing Editor | Donia Ann Steele |
| Director of Design | Christopher M. Register |

First Printing. Printed in Canada


TIME-LIFE is a trademark of Time Warner Inc. U.S.A.

Produced by Storey Communications, Inc.,
105 Schoolhouse Road, Pownal, Vermont 05261

| | |
|---|---|
| President | M. John Storey |
| Executive Vice President | Martha M. Storey |
| Vice President and Publisher | Pamela B. Art |
| Custom Publishing Director | Amanda R. Haar |
| Editors | Jeffrey D. Litton, Deirdre Lynch, and Angela Cardinali |
| Cover and Text Design | Black Trout Design, Carol J. Jessop |
| Layout and Text Production | Sarah Brill |
| Illustrations and Production Assistance | David C. Umlauf |
| Illustrations | Allyson Hayes |

Library of Congress Cataloging-in-Publication Data

Labinsky, Daria
    The brewpub cookbook : favorite recipes from great brewpub
kitchens / by Daria Labinsky and Stan Hieronymus.
        p.      cm.
    Includes index.
    ISBN 0-7835-4906-7
    1. Cookery    2. Beer—United States    3. Microbreweries—
United States.    I. Hieronymus, Stan.    II. Title.
TX714.L293    1997
641.5—dc21

                                        96-50877
                                        CIP

# DEDICATION

*We dedicate this book to all the brewers and chefs who believe making quality beer and food is more important than making lots of money.*

# ACKNOWLEDGMENTS

We raise our glasses in a toast to the owners, chefs, and other employees of the brewpubs whose recipes are included in *The Brewpub Cookbook*, and to those who sent recipes that we simply didn't have room for. We would also like to thank those journalists whose books and articles on beer helped us complete this book, especially Michael Jackson, Gregg Smith, and Marty Nachel. Special thanks to chef and writer Lucy Saunders.

Additionally, we would like to thank Rick Westervelt, Steve Johnson, David Furer and the participants in the Midwest Beer Expo's Brewpub Invitational, Ron and Sue Widdows, Bill Owens, Daniel Bradford, Jim Dorsch, Sara and Phil Doersam, Tim Harper, Craig Bystrynski, Bev and Don Walsmith, the editors at Storey Communications, Tom Peters, Christopher Demetri, the AbNormal Brewers, the Chicago Beer Society, all the Beer Travelers newsletter subscribers, our former Journal Star co-workers, A. A. Applegate, Steve King, our friends at Oldenberg Brewery's Beer Camp, Jane Miller, and our families, especially Irene Labinsky, who didn't complain no matter how many brewpubs we took her to, Gretchen and Mike Beall, Ryan, and Sierra.

# TABLE OF CONTENTS

**INTRODUCTION**

The Brewpub Explosion and Beer Cuisine. . . . . . . . . . . . . 1
The Basics of Beer. . . . . . . . . . . . . . . . . . . . . . . . . . . 2
Matching Beer with Food . . . . . . . . . . . . . . . . . . . . . . 3
Serving Beer . . . . . . . . . . . . . . . . . . . . . . . . . . . . . 6
About the Brewpubs and Recipes . . . . . . . . . . . . . . . . . 8

**CHAPTER 1** APPETIZERS AND SIDE DISHES

Smoked Chicken Nachos with Beer Cheese Sauce
 *Bluegrass Brewing Co., Louisville, KY* . . . . . . . . . . . 10
Bay Shrimp Pestodillas
 *Prescott Brewing Co., Prescott, AZ* . . . . . . . . . . . . 12
Mushroom Pâté
 *Crane River Brewpub & Cafe, Lincoln, NE.* . . . . . . . . 14
Vegetarian Strudel
 *75th Street Brewery, Kansas City, MO* . . . . . . . . . . . 16
Beer Cheese Spread
 *Wynkoop Brewing Co., Denver, CO.* . . . . . . . . . . . . 18
Crab and Artichoke Dip
 *The Wharf Rat Camden Yards, Baltimore, MD.* . . . . . . 19
Asiago Cheese Dip with Beer Bread
 *Walnut Brewery, Boulder, CO* . . . . . . . . . . . . . . . . 20
Black Bean Dip
 *Hunter–Gatherer Brewery, Columbia, SC* . . . . . . . . . 22

**CHAPTER 2** SANDWICHES AND PIZZAS

Veggie Pita
 *Mickey Finn's Brewery, Libertyville, IL* . . . . . . . . . . . 24
Grilled Chicken Sub
 *Hyde Park Brewing Co., Hyde Park, NY* . . . . . . . . . . 26
Chicken Bayou Sandwich
 *Fuggles Microbrewery, Salt Lake City, UT* . . . . . . . . . 28
Grilled Black Forest Ham and Gruyère Sandwich
 *The Black Rabbit Restaurant, Troutdale, OR* . . . . . . . . 30
Black-and-Blue Burger
 *Montgomery Brewing Co., Montgomery, AL* . . . . . . . . 31
Kennebunkport's Best Reuben
 *Federal Jack's Restaurant & Brewpub, Kennebunk, ME* . . 32
Pizza Acapulco
 *Brewmasters Pub, Restaurant, & Brewery, Kenosha, WI* . 34
The Fluke Pizza
 *Marin Brewing Co., Larkspur, CA* . . . . . . . . . . . . . 36
Chicken Cordon Bleu Pizza
 *Magic City Brewery, Birmingham, AL* . . . . . . . . . . . 38

**CHAPTER 3** SOUPS, CHILIS, AND STEWS

Crab and Corn Chowder
 *Capitol City Brewing Co., Washington, DC* . . . . . . . . 42
Smoked Salmon Chowder
 *Elm City Brewing Co., Keene, NH* . . . . . . . . . . . . . 44
Italian Chicken Tortellini Soup
 *Ebbets Field, Springfield, MO* . . . . . . . . . . . . . . . . 46

Beer and Cheese Soup
*Mill Rose Brewing Co., South Barrington, IL.* . . . . . . . . . 48
Seven Onion Soup
*The Church Brew Works, Pittsburgh, PA* . . . . . . . . . . . . 50
Iron Horse Stout Chili
*Big River Grille and Brewing Works, Chattanooga, TN.* . . 52
Vegetarian Green Chili Stew
*Eske's Brew Pub & Eatery, Taos, NM* . . . . . . . . . . . . . . 54
Jambalaya with Creole Sauce
*Empire Brewing Co., Syracuse, NY* . . . . . . . . . . . . . . . 56
Wheat Beer Potato Soup
*Hops! Bistro & Brewery, Scottsdale, AZ.* . . . . . . . . . . . 58

## CHAPTER 4  SALADS AND PASTA DISHES
Linguine Oasis
*Italian Oasis & Brewery, Littleton, NH.* . . . . . . . . . . . . 60
Fettuccine with Weissbier Cream
*Zip City Brewing Co., New York, NY* . . . . . . . . . . . . . . 61
Caesar Salad with Focaccia
*Il Vicino Wood Oven Pizza & Brewery, Salida, CO* . . . . 62
Grilled Vegetable Salad with Sesame-Ginger Vinaigrette
*Coppertank Brewing Co., Austin, TX* . . . . . . . . . . . . . . 64
Grilled Tuna Salad with Corn Relish and Peach Salsa
*Eddie McStiff's Restaurant and Micro Brewery, Moab, UT* 66
"Sonoma" Shrimp with Capellini Pasta
*Richbrau Brewing Co. and Restaurant, Richmond, VA.* . . 68
Penne Pasta
*Union Station Brewing Co., Providence, RI* . . . . . . . . . . 70
Spicy Angel Hair Pasta
*Ragtime Tavern & Grill, Atlantic Beach, FL.* . . . . . . . . . 72

## CHAPTER 5  SEAFOOD ENTRÉES
Spicy Beer Shrimp
*Mill Street Brewing Co., St. Paul, MN.* . . . . . . . . . . . . . 74
Fish and Chips
*Broad Ripple Brewpub, Indianapolis, IN* . . . . . . . . . . . 75
Braised Halibut with Vegetables and Herbs
*Pyramid Alehouse, Seattle, WA* . . . . . . . . . . . . . . . . . 76
Harvest Amber Ale BBQ Shrimp
*Flatlander's Chophouse and Brewery, Lincolnshire, IL* . . . 78
Dock Street Beer Seafood Fest
*Dock Street Brewing Co., Philadelphia, PA* . . . . . . . . . 80
Pumpkin-Spiced Salmon
*Boston Beer Works, Boston, MA* . . . . . . . . . . . . . . . . . 82
Caribbean Mango Tuna
*Olde Towne Tavern and Brewing Co., Gaithersburg, MD* 84
Spicy Beer-Steamed Mussels with Ancho Butter
*Grizzly Peak Brewing Co., Ann Arbor, MI.* . . . . . . . . . . 86

## CHAPTER 6  POULTRY ENTRÉES
Deep Enders Chicken
*Anderson Valley Brewing Co., Boonville, CA.* . . . . . . . . 90
Brewhouse Chicken Alfredo
*Randy's FunHunters Brewery, Whitewater, WI* . . . . . . . . 91
Braised Chicken in Weizen Ale
*Ozark Brewing Co., Fayetteville, AR.* . . . . . . . . . . . . . 92

Santa Fe Chicken
*North Coast Brewing Co., Fort Bragg, CA* . . . . . . . . . 94
Cock-A-Leekie Pie
*The Vermont Pub & Brewery, Burlington, VT* . . . . . . . . 96
Anasazi Chicken
*Cottonwood Grille & Brewery, Boone, NC.* . . . . . . . . 98
Orange-Cilantro Roasted Chicken
*Barley & Hopps Brewery, San Mateo, CA* . . . . . . . . 100
Grilled Chicken and Sweet Corn Risotto
*Triumph Brewing Co., Princeton, NJ.* . . . . . . . . . . . 100
Chicken Jalfrajie
*Jaipur Restaurant and Brewing Co., Omaha, NE* . . . . . 104

## CHAPTER 7  MEAT ENTRÉES
Italian Meat Balls
*Pete's Place, Krebs, OK.* . . . . . . . . . . . . . . . . . 106
Badlands Pork Tenderloin
*Rattlesnake Creek Brewery and Grill, Dickinson, ND* . . 107
Pork Rouladen with Düsseldorf Cream Sauce
*The Black Angus at Stoudt Brewery, Adamstown, PA* . . 108
Shepherd's Pie
*Gritty McDuff's Brew Pub, Portland, ME* . . . . . . . . . 110
Bavarian Pot Roast with Stout Gravy
*Leavenworth Brewery, Leavenworth, WA.* . . . . . . . . . 112
Beef with Black Radish Beer
*Weeping Radish Brewery, Manteo, NC.* . . . . . . . . . . 114
Spiessbraten
*Sudwerk Privatbrauerei Hübsch, Davis, CA* . . . . . . . . 116
Buffalo or Beef Brisket
*Firehouse Brewing Co., Rapid City, SD* . . . . . . . . . . 118
Baby Back Ribs with Stoddard's Brew BBQ Sauce
*Stoddard's Brewhouse & Eatery, Sunnyvale, CA.* . . . . . 120
Steak with Aloha Ale Sauce
*Gentleman Jim's Bistro and Brewery, Poughkeepsie, NY* 122

## CHAPTER 8  DESSERTS
Chocolate Truffles
*TableRock Brewpub & Grill, Boise, ID* . . . . . . . . . . . 124
The Double Triple
*Great Northern Restaurant & Brewery, Fargo, ND* . . . . 125
Chocolate Calzone
*Vino's Brewpub, Little Rock, AR* . . . . . . . . . . . . . . 126
Lemon-Orange Pudding Cake
*Gordon Biersch, Honolulu, HI* . . . . . . . . . . . . . . . 128
Chocolate Stout Torte
*Dempsey's Ale House, Petaluma, CA* . . . . . . . . . . . 130
Stout Cheesecake
*Commonwealth Brewing Co., Boston, MA.* . . . . . . . . . 132
Cascade Pumpkin Brûlée
*Goose Island Brewing Co., Chicago, IL.* . . . . . . . . . . 134
Black Stout Pecan Pie with Oatmeal Stout Ice Cream
*Phoenix Brewing Co., Atlanta, GA.* . . . . . . . . . . . . . 136
Toffee Pudding
*St. Louis Brewery and Tap Room, St. Louis, MO.* . . . . . 138

Appendix: Beer Styles and Commercial Examples . . . . . . . 139
Standard Index to Recipes. . . . . . . . . . . . . . . . . . . . 148
State-by-State Index . . . . . . . . . . . . . . . . . . . . . . . 152

# INTRODUCTION

## THE BREWPUB EXPLOSION
## AND BEER CUISINE

Bert Grant popped the top on the U.S. brewpub explosion in 1982 when he swung open the doors to Grant's Brewery Pub in Yakima, Washington. Seven years later, the United States was home to 100 brewery-restaurants. Over the next seven years, nearly 700 more brewpubs joined the crowd, and by the end of 1997, more than 1,000 will be operating in the United States.

The brewpub experience not only differs from other dining and drinking adventures, but usually differs from brewpub to brewpub. Brewpubs come in all shapes and sizes. River City Brewing Company in Jacksonville, Florida, spreads across 29,500 square feet, inside and out, while the Star Garnet Brewing Company in Boise, Idaho, opened in a former corner gas station. Many brewery-restaurants are located in historic buildings, and incorporate the existing architecture into their design.

The popularity of brewpubs mirrors a trend seen throughout late-20th century culture—the desire for something distinctive as opposed to something mass produced. Since you are reading this book, you are probably one of the many people who has grown to appreciate beer that's fuller in flavor than most of what is marketed by the world's mainstream, industrial brewers. And like many of these people, you seek out food that's a step beyond what you can get at the local chain restaurant. The brewpubs of today meet your needs by offering both fine beer and good food.

Although most of the first brewpubs featured basic "pub grub"—burgers, fried foods, hot wings, and the like—proprietors soon began to come up with more unusual menu items to emphasize the uniqueness of their pubs. Eventually, brewpub operators realized that brewpub cuisine can include anything and everything—from Chinese dim sum to pasta with goat cheese and sun-dried tomatoes.

While some brewpubs offer bills of fare that can be categorized as gourmet, many continue to serve food items that are variations on traditional American tavern foods, such as pizza and sandwiches. However, rather than pull something prepackaged out of the freezer, the new generation of brewpub chefs uses fresh ingredients in the preparation of these simple dishes, and many of their menus feature items designed to appeal to vegetarians and other health-conscious eaters. Fresh food goes with fresh beer, which is, after all, the brewpubs' selling point. The traditionalist will still find quarter- or half-pound burgers on the menu, but they're probably made with top-quality sirloin, or even with lamb or buffalo, and served on multigrain buns.

As the craft brewing movement has grown and matured, a new food style, called "beer cuisine," has evolved to accompany it. Chefs are learning how beer and food work together and how their flavors contrast with or complement one another, and they are preparing dishes specifically to match certain beers. Actually, the concept is not new; chefs in France and Belgium have been cooking with beer and matching it with food for years. Today, schools such as the Culinary Institute of America in Hyde Park, New York, and the College of Culinary Arts at Johnson & Wales University in Providence, Rhode Island, are educating their students about cooking with beer and matching beers with complementary foods. It's not uncommon for brewpubs to have professionally trained executive chefs on board.

## THE BASICS OF BEER

Beer is any fermented beverage made from grain and seasoned with hops or other bittering ingredients. According to the German purity law of 1516, known as the Reinheitsgebot (pronounced rhine-HEIGHTS-ga-boat), beer should only be made from malted barley or wheat, water, hops, and yeast.

Many breweries will use only the above ingredients to make beer. In the United States, however, where many microbrewers had their start as homebrewers, you'll find beer flavored with fruit, spices, syrups, and many other ingredients. These flavored beers do have the basic Reinheitsgebot ingredients as a base. The world's brewing giants add adjuncts to their beers, such as rice and corn, which are less expensive than malt and lighten the taste of beer.

By combining ingredients in varying amounts and different ways, a brewer can produce innumerable kinds of beer. The process of making beer, from mixing the ingredients to fermentation to storage, can take as little as two weeks, or, if you're a Belgian monk, as long as two years. Brewpub beers are not pasteurized, so freshness is key. The best brewpubs pride themselves on serving no beer after its time.

## KINDS OF BEER

Beer is divided into two basic categories, ales and lagers. An ale is a top-fermenting beer, which means the yeast rises to the top as it ferments. The vast majority of American craft breweries, including brewpubs, produce ales. Ales are more practical for a small brewer to make because they ferment more quickly than lagers, enabling the brewer to produce more beer in a shorter amount of time. The yeast used to make ales and the warm fermentation impart interesting flavor and aroma characteristics, such as fruitiness and floweriness. When compared to lagers, ales have a fuller taste. Generally speaking, ales are hoppy and strongly flavored.

A lager is a bottom-fermenting brew, which means the yeast falls to the bottom of the container during fermentation. Lagers generally look clearer than ales because the cold aging kills bacteria and cuts down on haze in the brew (not that haze and bacteria are necessarily bad). Lagers have a cleaner, crisper taste and are less fruity than ales. The flavors of lagers are often subtler than those of ales, although many lagers have a pronounced hoppiness or maltiness. For a detailed look at the different styles of beer, see the Appendix.

## MATCHING BEER WITH FOOD

Six months after opening its doors, Flatlander's Chophouse and Brewery in Lincolnshire, Illinois, was already serving an average of 1,000 meals a day. Accommodating large crowds was nothing new to kitchen manager Mike Schrafel, who had worked in corporate food service for 10 years. But preparing food to accompany beer and cooking with beer were uncharted waters for him. Brainstorming for new menu items or daily specials is an ongoing process at the brewpub. Twice a week, Schrafel sits down with supervisors to toss ideas around.

"I take a recipe that sounds good and wonder what I can do to modify it," Schrafel said. Often, the secret ingredient is beer. For example, Schrafel made a warm German potato salad, but the salad was lacking something. At the brewmaster's suggestion, he added Oktoberfest lager and a bit of spicy mustard to the salad. The marriage of the potato salad to the beer and mustard gave the dish a delicious, tangy kick.

Creativity and a willingness to take chances are the keys to cooking with beer. They're also important when it comes to deciding which beers to serve with which foods. Matching food with beer is not an exact science—think of it instead as a delicious, ever-evolving experiment.

Alan Skversky, regional executive chef for the Arizona-based Hops! Bistro & Brewery restaurants, began incorporating beer into food when he joined Hops! in May 1994. The learning process has been one of trial and error. "There are no set rules," he said. "We've been trying to standardize, but every time we try a different beer with a different food, we're blown away by the possibilities."

However, there are some basic guidelines a cook can follow. The keywords to serving beer with food are "cut," "complement," and "contrast." You may want to cut a dish that is very rich or buttery by serving it with a light, hoppy beer such as a pilsner. A perfect complement to anything chocolate-flavored is stout. And a pale ale will contrast with the hearty, smoky flavors of a barbecue dish.

A good rule of thumb is to start with any beer you like, and move on from there. Be aware, however, that some matches are not made in heaven. Just as you cannot follow certain kinds of beers with others in a beer tasting (general rule: go from least to most hoppy), you cannot always appreciate the full flavor of certain beers if you've preceded them with the wrong food. A bite of Limburger or other strong cheese, for example, can change the flavor of just about any beer that will follow. Often, drinking the wrong beer with food will detract from the flavor of the food as well.

Beer goes well with many intensely flavored foods, including smoked meats and dishes in which the herbs and spices are strong, such as a hot curry dish, a plate of barbecue, or Tex-Mex cuisine. Beer can refresh your mouth after it has encountered such strong flavors. You can complement strongly flavored foods with strongly flavored beers. For example,

Skversky noted that a spicy shrimp dish will taste even spicier with a hoppy ale. Or you can mellow out the intensity by serving a Vienna lager or Oktoberfest, or even a light pilsner. For super-hot food, such as blackened redfish or Szechuan shrimp, stick to an American pilsner, lager, or wheat beer. Once your tongue has been assaulted with hot spices, it will no longer be able to appreciate a more intricately flavored beer. And a richer beer may detract from the food's flavors. One basic guideline is to match ethnic cuisine with beers of the same country. Try German bratwurst and hot mustard with a German dark lager, English stout with steak-and-kidney pie, English brown ales or bitters with mild sausage, or a hoppy American pale ale or pilsner with steamed clams.

Stouts and porters also go well with shellfish. With fried or broiled fish, try a hoppy pilsner or pale ale, and with smoked fish, a malty ale. For sauced chicken or pork dishes, a malty beer such as a Vienna-style lager, bock, Oktoberfest, or Munich-style dark lager will work well. Light chicken dishes, however, go better with a light lager, pilsner, or wheat beer. Lamb, beef, and game match with ales that have a fruity character, such as pale ales or English-style bitters.

Quite a few recipes in *The Brewpub Cookbook* are prepared with beer. But just because you're making a dish with beer doesn't mean you must serve that beer with it. Often, you'll want to serve a beer that has the opposite characteristics of the one with which you cooked. For example, Skversky finds the yeasty hefeweiss that is used in Hops! Wheat Beer Potato Soup (page 58) too "palate-coating" to accompany the soup, and he prefers to serve it with a light golden ale. However, everyone's palate is different, and other folks think the hefeweiss is a great match for the soup.

If you're planning a beer dinner, with a different beer for each course, you'll need to consider not only how each beer will go with each food item, but how the different beers will follow one another. Don't serve rich, heavy beers, or beers made with herbs and spices with your first few courses.

5

The guidelines are constantly evolving, as creative brewers develop increasingly varied kinds of beer. What should you serve with an apricot ale, for example, or an espresso stout? It falls to chefs skilled in beer cuisine to find just the right food to go with any style of beer.

Once you start experimenting with beer and food pairings, you'll quickly discover that not only does beer enhance the flavor of food, but food enhances the flavor of beer. You will start to pick up the many complexities that beer has hidden within it, and as you educate your palate, you'll begin to develop ideal beer and food pairings on your own.

## SERVING BEER

If you sit down at an Irish pub bar and ask for a stout, the publican will pour you what looks like a pint glass filled with foam. In a few seconds, the foam will dissipate from the bottom up, like a reverse waterfall, until you're left facing a deep-brown glass of beer with a perfect head. The presentation is as much a part of enjoying the beer as is the beer itself, which is why beer can best be sampled when it's served in the proper glass.

Why not just drink beer from the bottle? A beer served in a glass will be properly carbonated, while beer drunk straight from the bottle is higher in carbonation. Also, the beauty of beer can be better appreciated when seen through a clear glass, as opposed to a colored-glass bottle. Thirdly, the aroma of the beer is fuller when sniffed from a glass.

That certain styles of beer are best served in certain kinds of glassware is partly historical, partly aesthetic, and partly common sense. What follows are some general guidelines.

Most ales are best served in pint glasses. The head is easy to see and appreciate. Pint glasses come with straight sides, sides that are bowled at the top, sides with a bulge at the half-pint point, and as handled mugs. All pint glasses share a wide mouth.

Strong ales, such as barley wines and some stronger stouts, should be served in small-stemmed glasses. Small, because the beer has a higher alcohol content; stemmed, so you can twirl it in your fingers and catch the complex aroma.

Belgian ales are often served in tulip-shaped, stemmed goblets. When properly poured, the top of the tulip holds the head.

Wheat beers require very tall glasses (because they're usually bottled in larger sizes) that are bowled out at the top, the better to capture the huge head. Since a fruit beer is more likely to be sipped than quaffed, it is often served in a small glass that looks like a champagne flute without the stem.

Lagers are often served in tall, tapered glasses, called pilsener glasses because they came from Plzen in what is today the Czech Republic. They are designed to let you appreciate the bubbles rising up from the bottom of the glass (indicating freshness) and the delicate lacework that clings to the sides of the glass. Because the glass is narrow, the tall head will linger longer.

Of course, no one needs to run out and buy all of these different kinds of glassware. If you're going to purchase just one beer glass, determine which style of beer you most prefer and buy accordingly. If you're an ale fan, go with the pint glass; a lager lover, the pilsener glass. For strong beers, wine glasses work fine. Some beer judges recommend brandy snifters, because their narrow-mouthed bowl best captures the aroma. The most important thing to look for in a general-use beer glass is that it will hold 12 to 16 ounces, so it can accommodate an entire bottle of beer. You may want to purchase British imperial pint glasses, which hold 20 ounces, but a glass that holds more than the amount of beer poured will lose its head more quickly.

Devout beer lovers recommend using baking soda, rather than soap, to wash beer glasses. Soap can leave a film that you may not see, and may affect the beer's head retention.

The proper temperature is essential to beer enjoyment. A beer served too cold will withhold most of its flavor, while one served too warm will go flat quickly. Some general guidelines:

Serve fruit beers at 40°F–50°F.

Serve wheat beers and pale lagers at 40°F–45°F.

Serve pale ales and amber or dark lagers at 45°F–55°F.

Serve strong ales, such as barley wines and Belgian ales, at 50°F–60°F.

Serve dark ales, including porters and stouts, at 50°F–55°F.

## ABOUT THE BREWPUBS AND RECIPES

The restaurants that contributed recipes to the book range from cozy, traditional British-style pubs to spacious, high-tech trendy joints. Some of them have been in business for years, while many others are newer brewpubs that have already established reputations for quality food and beer. Some of the chefs whose work is featured are professionally trained artists who showcase their talents by designing cutting-edge cuisine, while others favor more downhome fare. Quite a few, naturally, use beer as an ingredient in their dishes, and a few incorporate raw ingredients that go into beer—hops and malt—into their recipes. Others focus on preparing food that isn't made with beer, but tastes good alongside the beers that their brewpubs serve.

Each recipe is accompanied by a recommended beer pairing. Many of the brewpubs listed in the book are also bottling microbreweries, and their chefs recommend using or serving their own beer. Since not all of the beer is widely available, see the Appendix for suggested beers in the same style. If you're fortunate enough to live in a town where a brewpub is located, and where it's legal for them to sell off premise, you may want to purchase fresh beer from your local pub.

## A NOTE FROM THE AUTHORS

We live in the country outside Peoria, Illinois, an industrial Midwestern city not known for gourmet cuisine. If we could not find an ingredient used in the cookbook within 20 miles of our house, we suggested an appropriate substitution.

CHAPTER 1

# APPETIZERS AND SIDE DISHES

I n the old days, "appetizers" used to be just that—
morsels of food meant to pique your appetite and
stimulate hunger for the rest of the meal. But in the
1980s, the concept of "grazing" took off.

Today, it's fairly common for a diner to opt for one
or two appetizers and forgo an entrée. This idea
makes sense when you're eating at a brewpub. For
all its charms, beer can be filling. Having a pint along with
an appetizer or while sharing a bowl of dip and crudités is a
way to combat that "too full" feeling from a complete meal.

Of course, it's perfectly all right to eat an appetizer and
move on to a main course. Remember to stay away from
full-bodied, rich beers with appetizers if you plan to drink
more beer later in the meal.

In addition to appetizers and dips, this chapter also
includes a few side dishes, such as beer bread and strudel,
that work well with recipes featured in later chapters. When
deciding which beers to serve with them, you'll need to
consider what kind of beer will go with the entrée.

# SMOKED CHICKEN NACHOS WITH BEER CHEESE SAUCE

## BLUEGRASS BREWING CO., LOUISVILLE, KY

*Nachos appear on many brewpub menus. These are more flavorful than many others, because they feature smoked chicken, and the cheese sauce is made with beer. Serve them with a hoppy pale ale.*

## BEER CHEESE SAUCE

1 cup chicken broth

1 cup red ale

½ cup whole milk

1 tablespoon vegetable seasoning (such as Mrs. Dash)

½ onion, diced small

2 jalapeños, diced small

1 teaspoon puréed or granulated garlic

White pepper to taste

1½ pounds American cheese, sliced

½ cup cold water

½ cup cornstarch

YIELD: 4 SERVINGS

# NACHOS

Corn or flour tortilla chips
1 cup canned black beans
Salt, pepper, and chili powder to taste
$\frac{1}{2}$ pound smoked or cooked chicken breast, diced
1 cup shredded lettuce
1 cup chopped fresh tomatoes
$\frac{1}{2}$ cup chopped green onions
$\frac{1}{2}$ cup sliced black olives
$\frac{1}{4}$ cup sliced canned jalapeños, or to taste
(can substitute fresh jalapeños)
$\frac{1}{2}$ cup sour cream
$\frac{1}{2}$ cup guacamole (optional)

1. Prepare Beer Cheese Sauce: In a large pot, combine chicken broth, beer, milk, seasoning, onion, jalapeños, garlic, and pepper. Simmer for 15 minutes.

2. Over very low heat, add 1 slice of American cheese at a time, whisking constantly. Do not leave unattended. After all the cheese is melted and whisked in, remove the pot from heat.

3. In a separate bowl, whisk together the cornstarch and water. Add cornstarch mixture in a slow stream to the Beer Cheese Sauce, whisking constantly. Add just enough cornstarch mixture to bring sauce to a nice consistency.

4. Prepare Nachos: Drain and rinse black beans. Heat over low heat and season with salt, pepper, and chili powder to taste.

5. Cover four individual small plates or one large platter with tortilla chips. Pour heated black beans over chips. Add diced chicken. Cover with hot Beer Cheese Sauce. Top with shredded lettuce, tomatoes, green onions, olives, and jalapeños. Add a dollop of sour cream and guacamole to the top of the nachos. Serve warm with extra Beer Cheese Sauce on the side.

# BAY SHRIMP PESTODILLAS

## PRESCOTT BREWING CO., PRESCOTT, AZ

*A variation on Mexican quesadillas, Bay Shrimp Pestodillas bring together a hint of Italian pesto and tasty bay shrimp morsels for an ample appetizer that can be shared among friends. Prepared as directed, it melds a perfect blend of flavors. Prescott Brewing suggests a light and refreshing fruit beer with this dish, such as a wheat beer garnished with a slice of lemon or an American-brewed apricot ale.*

4 10-inch flour tortillas
$\frac{1}{2}$ cup pesto sauce (available in most supermarkets)
$\frac{1}{2}$ pound mozzarella cheese, shredded
1 pound bay shrimp (180-250 count is desirable), cooked, peeled, and deveined
$\frac{1}{4}$ head green leaf lettuce, shredded
Garnish: diced tomatoes, chopped fresh cilantro, sour cream, guacamole, salsa

1. Preheat oven to 350°F. Warm tortillas. Warm pesto sauce, and ladle 2 tablespoons over each tortilla.

2. Spread $\frac{1}{4}$ of the mozzarella cheese over each tortilla. Spread $\frac{1}{4}$ of the bay shrimp over each tortilla. Top with about $\frac{1}{4}$ of the shredded lettuce.

3. Fold tortilla and place on sheet pan. Bake for about 5 minutes, or until cheese is melted.

4. Cut each tortilla into 4 or 5 triangular pieces, and arrange around a large platter with points facing outward. Garnish with diced tomatoes and remaining lettuce or chopped fresh cilantro. Serve with sour cream, guacamole, and salsa.

**YIELD: 4–6 SERVINGS AS AN APPETIZER**

# MUSHROOM PÂTÉ

## CRANE RIVER BREWPUB & CAFE, LINCOLN, NE

*Located in downtown Lincoln, Crane River is a spacious, open brewpub. On one wall is a beautiful quilted wall hanging from a local artist depicting Nebraska's famous Platte River cranes. Wheat beer, cream cheese, and mushrooms combine to give this appetizer a rich earthy flavor and creamy texture that will appeal to aficionados of pâté de fois gras and vegetarians alike. It's great for preparing ahead, because it keeps well for a week or two if refrigerated and tightly covered. This dish is especially nice after the theater, matched with a glass of porter.*

1¾ pounds white button mushrooms
½ yellow onion, chopped
1 pound cream cheese, softened
2 cloves garlic
2 teaspoons paprika
2 teaspoons dill weed
1½ teaspoons salt
1 teaspoon white pepper
⅓ cup lightly hopped American-style wheat beer
Lettuce leaves
Water crackers

1. Preheat oven to 350°F. Thoroughly wash mushrooms. Purée mushrooms and onions in a food processor or blender.

2. Place the mushroom purée in a saucepan with the onion, garlic, and spices. Add the beer, and cook until the liquid evaporates.

3. Put softened cream cheese in a mixing bowl, and mix until smooth. Add the mushroom mixture, and mix on low speed until the pâté is free of lumps and creamy in texture.

4. Spray a 9x9 baking pan with nonstick cooking spray. Place mushroom mixture in the pan, and bake for 30–40 minutes. Remove from the oven and cool completely.

5. Stir pâté thoroughly before use. Serve cold, mounded on a lettuce leaf with water crackers as an accompaniment.

YIELD: 8 APPETIZER SERVINGS

# VEGETARIAN STRUDEL

## 75TH STREET BREWERY, KANSAS CITY, MO

*This strudel is made of buttery phyllo dough (available in the frozen section of most supermarkets) wrapped around a delicious combination of woodland mushrooms, roasted red pepper, spinach, and mozzarella cheese. 75th Street serves the strudel as an entrée with chilled couscous and tomato coulis and teamed with a salad. It is an easy yet elegant choice for spring brunch. Serve it with a light beer, such as a wheat beer.*

### FILLING

1 red pepper

4 tablespoons olive oil, plus oil for brushing pepper

1 medium onion, diced

$\frac{1}{3}$ pound shiitake mushrooms, sliced

$\frac{1}{3}$ pound crimini mushrooms, sliced

1 garlic clove, minced

$\frac{3}{4}$ pound spinach, cleaned and de-stemmed

1. Brush red pepper with olive oil and place directly on a gas stove burner. (If a gas burner is not available, an electric broiler will work as well.) Cook and turn pepper until skin is evenly blackened. Place pepper in a bowl, tightly cover with plastic wrap, and set aside.

2. Heat 2 tablespoons olive oil in a heavy, large, non-stick skillet over medium-high heat. Add onions, and sauté until they become fragrant, less than a minute. Add mushrooms, and allow to cook about 8 minutes or until tender. Transfer mushroom mixture to a bowl.

3. Add remaining 2 tablespoons oil to same skillet over medium high heat. Add minced garlic, and sauté until brown. Lower heat to medium. Add spinach, turning until it begins to wilt. Remove spinach from heat, and transfer to another bowl.

4. Once red pepper has cooled, remove plastic wrap from the bowl and cut off top and bottom of the pepper. Cut pepper lengthwise, remove seeds and black skin, and cut into thin strips.

## STRUDEL ASSEMBLY

8 sheets phyllo pastry, thawed
6 tablespoons butter, melted
6 ounces mozzarella, drained, or
low-moisture mozzarella, thinly sliced
2 tablespoons chopped parsley

1. Preheat oven to 375°F. Place one pastry sheet on work surface. Brush with melted butter, and sprinkle pastry sheet with some of the parsley. Lay second sheet of pastry over the first, and repeat process until you have a stack of eight sheets.

2. Place phyllo on the work surface with the long side toward you. Begin to layer spinach, then mushrooms, red pepper, and cheese in a 4-inch strip, 3 inches from the bottom and 2 inches in from the sides. Carefully fold short ends of pastry over filling. Fold 3-inch border over filling and begin to roll. Place strudel seam side down on a baking sheet lined with parchment paper, and brush with butter.

3. Bake strudel until golden brown, about 25 minutes. Remove from oven, cool slightly, and slice strudel on an angle.

YIELD: 4 SERVINGS

# BEER CHEESE SPREAD

## WYNKOOP BREWING CO., DENVER, CO

*This is a great holiday cheese spread that is quick and easy to prepare. Any full-bodied ale, including Wynkoop's bottled Railyard Ale, can be used to make it. Serve it with crackers, warm pretzels, or beer bread and the same beer that was used to make the spread. You may roll the chilled cheese mixture into a ball or log shape and then roll it in chopped nuts.*

6 ounces cream cheese, softened

6 ounces blue cheese, softened

12 ounces sharp white cheddar cheese, grated

$\frac{1}{4}$ cup minced green onions

1 teaspoon paprika

$\frac{1}{2}$ teaspoon celery seed

$\frac{1}{2}$ teaspoon ground black pepper

$\frac{1}{2}$ teaspoon Tabasco sauce

$\frac{1}{2}$ cup full-bodied ale

1. Combine all ingredients except beer in the bowl of a food processor or electric mixer. Mix or blend until everything is well incorporated.

2. Slowly add beer while processor or mixer is running. Place mixture into a crock or serving bowl, and chill until firm.

**YIELD: 1$\frac{1}{2}$ POUNDS**

# CRAB AND ARTICHOKE DIP

## THE WHARF RAT CAMDEN YARDS, BALTIMORE, MD

*Artichoke dip can be found on many brewpub menus. This one stands out because it uses that Maryland staple, crabmeat. It can be made a day or two in advance. Serve it with crudités, crackers, or toasted sourdough bread cubes, and a pale ale.*

$\frac{1}{2}$ pound lump crabmeat

1 can fancy artichoke hearts (8-10 count)

3 cloves garlic

1 pound cream cheese, softened

2 cups grated Parmesan cheese

1 cup mayonnaise

1. Purée garlic cloves in a food processor or blender. Drain artichokes and add to garlic. Process garlic and artichokes until well mixed. Add the cream cheese, and blend until completely smooth.

2. In a separate bowl, sort crabmeat, removing any shells. Add the cream cheese–artichoke mixture, Parmesan cheese, and mayonnaise. Stir until thoroughly combined. Serve hot.

YIELD: 8–12 SERVINGS

# ASIAGO CHEESE DIP WITH BEER BREAD

## WALNUT BREWERY, BOULDER, CO

*This brewpub is the original member of the Rock Bottom chain of brewpubs, which stretches across the country. Both of these recipes are very easy to prepare. The Asiago Cheese Dip is a delicious, hot, bubbly dip that makes you want more with every bite. Asiago is a dry, salty cheese. It's intensely flavored, and a little goes a long way. The Beer Bread is a dense, heavy loaf with a crunchy-chewy crust. It should be lightly toasted on both sides before serving with the dip. You may want to place the slices on a cookie sheet and slide them under the broiler, turning them over as they brown. Walnut Brewery suggests serving a brown, red, or other medium-bodied ale. You can use any kind of unsweetened beer in the bread recipe.*

## ASIAGO CHEESE DIP

1 cup mayonnaise

1 cup sour cream

½ cup plus 1 tablespoon shredded Asiago cheese

¼ cup green onions, cleaned, rinsed, and sliced

¼ cup mushrooms, rinsed and sliced

¼ cup sun-dried tomatoes

1. Preheat oven to 350°F. Reconstitute sun-dried tomatoes in hot water. Squeeze all the water out of the tomatoes, then julienne.

2. Combine all ingredients except tomatoes and 1 tablespoon of cheese. Fold in tomatoes. (Adding the tomatoes last prevents the dip from turning pink.)

3. Place in an oven-proof container and top with remaining 1 tablespoon cheese. Bake for about 15 minutes, or until bubbly. Serve immediately with toasted Beer Bread.

**YIELD: $3\frac{1}{4}$ CUPS**

## BEER BREAD

$\frac{1}{4}$ cup shredded cheddar cheese
1 cup sliced green onions
$\frac{3}{4}$ cup sugar
2 tablespoons salt
4 cups beer
8 cups flour
2 tablespoons baking powder
Oil as needed

1. Preheat oven to 350°F. Spray 2 loaf pans with nonstick cooking spray.

2. Mix cheese, green onions, sugar, and salt together.

3. In a separate bowl, mix flour and baking powder together.

4. Add beer to cheese mixture.

5. Add flour mixture, and mix by hand until thoroughly combined.

6. Place in loaf pans, and brush with oil. Bake for 10–15 minutes. (If you have a convection oven, keep fans on for this period.) Rotate bread, and finish baking (with fans off) for 40–45 minutes.

**YIELD: 2 LARGE LOAVES**

# BLACK BEAN DIP

## HUNTER-GATHERER BREWERY, COLUMBIA, SC

*Masks and other African artifacts decorate the walls of this brewpub. Serve this snacking fare with tortilla chips or pita triangles and a refreshing wheat ale.*

3 tablespoons olive oil
1 medium onion, diced
1 bell pepper, diced
5 jalapeños, seeded and diced
5 cloves garlic, peeled and diced
Juice of 1 lime
1 15-ounce can black beans, drained
1 medium tomato, cubed
$\frac{1}{4}$ pound cheddar cheese, shredded
(reserve some for garnish)
Garnish: Sour cream, 1 bunch green onions, chopped,
shredded cheddar cheese

1. Combine olive oil, onion, bell pepper, jalapeños, and garlic in a large sauté pan over medium heat. Squeeze lime juice over mixture in pan, and cook until onions become transluscent.

2. Reduce heat to low, and add black beans, tomato, and cheese (reserving some for garnish). Continue cooking until cheese melts and beans are heated through.

3. Garnish with a dollop of sour cream, shredded cheese, and chopped green onions.

**YIELD: 5–6 SERVINGS**

CHAPTER 2

# SANDWICHES AND PIZZAS

One of the nice things about sandwiches is their ease of preparation. Get a few rolls, slice some vegetables, layer on the meat, and in a matter of minutes you have a hearty meal. Sandwiches are incredibly versatile and lend themselves to experimentation. You can mix and match any number of ingredients, gussy-up the filling with a spicy dressing, or substitute a tasty bread for a roll. The sandwiches included here offer choices for vegetarians and meat-eaters alike. In some cases, you can prepare components of the sandwich—chop the vegetables in Mickey Finn's Veggie Pita, for example—in advance.

Many brewpubs offer some sort of pizza on their menu, often as an appetizer. There's something about the combination of spicy sauce, cheese, and crust that makes you crave a thirst-quenching brew, and pizza can stand up to most any kind of beer. The recipes here veer away from the usual tomato-and-cheese pizza, featuring instead such ingredients as chicken, pesto, and sun-dried tomatoes. You can make the pizzas in relatively little time if you start with store-bought pizza crust, but we've also included a homemade crust recipe that can be used with any of the pizza recipes in this chapter.

# VEGGIE PITA

## MICKEY FINN'S BREWERY, LIBERTYVILLE, IL

*When a patron is unsure of what to order, Mickey Finn's staff recommends this sandwich. You can add or subtract vegetables to your liking. The brewpub says it goes well with any of its beers, but something light, such as a golden ale or wheat beer, will pair nicely with the delicate flavors of the vegetables.*

$\frac{1}{2}$ pound mushrooms, halved

4 large zucchini, cut into long strips

4 large yellow squash, cut into long strips

2 large red peppers, seeded and cut into long strips

2 large green peppers, seeded and cut into long strips

2 large onions, sliced

$\frac{1}{4}$ cup butter

1 cup teriyaki sauce

$\frac{1}{2}$ head lettuce, shredded

2 large tomatoes, chopped

4 rounds of pita bread

4 slices mozzarella cheese

**YIELD: 4 SANDWICHES**

1. Melt butter in large skillet on high heat. Add mushrooms, zucchini, yellow squash, red pepper, green pepper, and onion. Sauté until almost tender. Add lettuce, tomato, and teriyaki sauce to the vegetable mixture for the last 1–2 minutes of cooking.

2. While the vegetables are sautéing, top each round of pita with a slice of mozzarella cheese. Warm pita bread and cheese in another skillet, until the bread is warm and the cheese is melted.

3. Divide vegetables into 4 portions. Top each pita with vegetables. Serve open-faced.

# GRILLED CHICKEN SUB

## HYDE PARK BREWING CO., HYDE PARK, NY

*This sandwich is extremely popular at the brewpub. The staff there uses a charbroiler, but a gas grill or sauté pan will work just fine. A fresh garden salad with a light dressing accompanies this sandwich nicely. A crisp pale ale will round out all the flavors.*

$\frac{3}{4}$ cup Dijon mustard

6 tablespoons Pommery or whole-grain mustard

$\frac{1}{4}$ cup yellow mustard

$1\frac{1}{2}$ teaspoons Worcestershire sauce

$\frac{1}{4}$ tablespoon Tabasco sauce

$\frac{1}{3}$ cup mayonnaise

1 pound fresh chicken breast, cut in half
and pounded slightly

2 6-inch sub rolls, sliced

2-ounce jar roasted red peppers, drained and julienned

4 slices Swiss cheese

1. Whisk together mustards, Worcestershire sauce, Tabasco, and mayonnaise to form marinade. Set aside 2 tablespoons of marinade to garnish the subs. Place chicken in marinade, and refrigerate overnight.

2. Preheat oven to 350°F. Grill or sauté marinated chicken for 2–3 minutes on each side. Top chicken with red peppers and the Swiss cheese. Place in oven until cheese melts.

3. Spread reserved marinade on sub rolls, and place chicken on rolls. Subs can be preassembled, and then placed in the oven to toast the sub rolls.

YIELD: 2 SANDWICHES

# CHICKEN BAYOU SANDWICH

## FUGGLES MICROBREWERY, SALT LAKE CITY, UT

*If spicy ham is not available, you can season regular ham with any Cajun-type spice seasoning. The chicken will take about nine minutes to cook. If the bread crumbs are too dark and the breast is not all the way cooked, place the chicken in the oven to finish cooking. Serve with a hoppy red ale.*

1 egg

2 tablespoons milk

2 tablespoons butter or oil

1 6-ounce boneless, skinless chicken breast

1 cup seasoned bread crumbs

3 ounces spicy ham, sliced thin

2 slices hot pepper jack cheese

1 tablespoon mayonnaise

1 hamburger bun

YIELD: 1 SERVING

1. Mix the egg and milk, and beat until combined.

2. In a hot sauté pan, add butter or oil. Place the chicken breast in the egg wash and then into the bread crumbs. Press the bread crumbs onto the chicken. Add the chicken breast to the hot sauté pan, and turn down the heat a little so it won't burn. Turn the breast as needed.

3. When the breast is almost cooked, place the ham in the pan with the chicken. When the ham is hot, layer it on top of the chicken breast. Place the slices of cheese on top of the ham, and cover the pan so that the cheese will melt.

4. Spread the mayonnaise on the bottom of the bun. Place the chicken, ham, and cheese on the bun, cut and serve.

# GRILLED BLACK FOREST HAM AND GRUYÈRE SANDWICH

## THE BLACK RABBIT RESTAURANT AT EDGEFIELD MANOR, TROUTDALE, OR

*Edgefield Manor is the showplace of the Pacific Northwest's McMenamins pub and brewpub chain. At the Black Rabbit, this sandwich is served on house-baked beer bread made with Terminator Stout. Gruyère is a nutty, hard cheese that originates in Switzerland. Complement with a porter or stout.*

### RED ONION–SAGE MARMALADE

2 tablespoons clarified butter

1 medium red onion, julienned

½ cup light ale

¼ cup brown sugar

1 tablespoon chopped fresh sage

1 teaspoon caraway seeds

1 tablespoon mustard seeds


½ pound Black Forest ham, thinly sliced

2 ounces Gruyère cheese, sliced

4 slices dark beer bread or pumpernickel

Garnish: Hard-boiled egg, green onion, spiced apple

1. Prepare Red Onion–Sage Marmalade: Melt butter. Cook onion in butter over low heat until caramelized. Add ale and brown sugar; reduce until thick. Add sage, caraway, and mustard seeds. Heat thoroughly.

2. Divide ham and cheese evenly on two slices of bread. Top with Marmalade and remaining bread slices. Grill sandwiches until cheese is melted. Garnish plate with hard-boiled egg, green onion, and spiced apple.

**YIELD: 2 SANDWICHES**

# BLACK-AND-BLUE BURGER

## MONTGOMERY BREWING CO., MONTGOMERY, AL

*Montgomery's warehouse district is home to this spacious brewpub, set in a historic building. The exposed brick walls set off the long bar, which overlooks the brewing equipment. This "blackened blue burger" is easy to make. At Montgomery Brewing, it's served with beer-batter fries and a red ale, but the blend of spices will work well with any red ale or amber ale or lager. Blackening retains the meat's juices and is best done on an outdoor grill. If you're cooking inside, keep the windows open and the overhead fan on high.*

½ pound hamburger
Blackening seasoning of your choice (such as K-Paul's)
1–2 ounces blue cheese, crumbled
Sesame seed bun
Garnish: Kosher pickle, lettuce, tomato

1. Liberally coat both sides of hamburger with seasoning, and sear in hot iron skillet.

2. Top with blue cheese to taste. Serve on sesame seed bun, garnished with pickle, lettuce, and tomato.

YIELD: 1 SERVING

# KENNEBUNKPORT'S BEST REUBEN

## FEDERAL JACK'S RESTAURANT & BREWPUB, KENNEBUNK, ME

*Former President George Bush has eaten this reuben often, says Charles Auger, Federal Jack's general manager. Federal Jack's is a partner with Kennebunkport Brewing Co., maker of Shipyard Ales, which are available in every state east of the Mississippi River. The brewpub makes the sauerkraut for this reuben, and recommends serving the sandwich with Shipyard Export Ale, a full-bodied, golden ale. If it's available in your area, feel free to use it; otherwise, substitute another golden ale. You'll have plenty of sauerkraut left over. It will keep in the refrigerator for up to six months.*

2 slices pumpernickel bread

Softened butter

5 ounces corned beef, sliced thin

2 slices Swiss cheese

$\frac{1}{4}$ cup Thousand Island dressing

6 tablespoons Beer-Braised Sauerkraut (see recipe at right)

1. Prepare Beer-Braised Sauerkraut.

2. Butter pumpernickel slices on both sides and toast well on a griddle. Place a slice of Swiss cheese on each piece of bread. Top with Thousand Island dressing.

3. In a nonstick or lightly oiled skillet, sauté corned beef until warmed through. Place on top of dressing.

4. Place Beer-Braised Sauerkraut on top of corned beef. Top with remaining slice of bread.

# BEER-BRAISED SAUERKRAUT

(Makes 2 pounds)

2 pounds fresh green cabbage, chopped

1 22-ounce bottle Shipyard Export Ale,
or other golden ale

1 teaspoon dried fennel

$\frac{1}{2}$ teaspoon black pepper

$\frac{3}{4}$ cup red wine vinegar

1. Combine all ingredients in a soup kettle or braising pan. Cook for 1 hour on low heat. Drain before serving.

YIELD: 1 SANDWICH

# PIZZA ACAPULCO

## BREWMASTERS PUB, RESTAURANT, & BREWERY KENOSHA, WI

*Brewmasters was one of the first brewpubs to open in Wisconsin. It is set inside a former stable for show horses and has a horseshoe-shaped bar. Warm colors give it a cozy feeling. Most beers taste great with pizza, but with this particular pizza a fruit beer would not be recommended. You can make your own pizza crust (see Magic City's on page 40), or buy ready-to-cook pizza crust or pizza dough at the store. A squeeze of fresh lemon on the avocado will keep it from discoloring.*

1 14-inch pizza crust

1 large clove garlic

2 tablespoons olive oil

1¼ cups salsa (homemade or bottled)

1 pound Monterey jack/cheddar cheese blend, shredded

½ pound chorizo or Italian sausage

10 black olives, sliced

10 green olives, sliced

1 avocado, sliced

YIELD: 2 SERVINGS AS AN ENTRÉE OR
4 SERVINGS AS AN APPETIZER

1. Preheat oven to 400°F. Press crust into lightly oiled pizza pan.

2. Crush garlic clove in garlic press or pulverize on a cutting board. Mix into olive oil. Brush garlic oil onto pizza crust with pastry brush.

3. Spread salsa evenly over crust, leaving $\frac{1}{2}$ inch uncovered around edge of pizza.

4. Top with cheese, followed by small pieces of uncooked chorizo or Italian sausage, and then olives.

5. Bake for 10–15 minutes.

6. Top with avocado slices. Slice and serve.

# THE FLUKE PIZZA

## MARIN BREWING CO., LARKSPUR, CA

*This pizza is the best-selling pizza at Marin Brewing and has been mentioned on local radio stations as one of the finest pizzas in the Bay Area. It's named for its creator, Chef Matt Fluke. If you plan to make your own pizza dough, Fluke recommends using equal parts semolina and all-purpose flour. If you wish, you can marinate the chicken in a soy sauce marinade before grilling. The pizza tastes great whether cooked in a wood-fired or regular oven. Serve it with an amber or pale ale.*

$\frac{1}{2}$ pound pizza dough

1 chicken breast

1 cup sliced mushrooms

Olive oil

$\frac{1}{4}$ cup pesto sauce

2 cups shredded mozzarella cheese

2 medium onions, sliced

1 cup crumbled feta cheese

1. Preheat oven to 375°F. Grease a cookie sheet, and put it in the oven.

2. On a floured board, roll dough into a 12-inch circle. Lightly pinch the edge all around to help form the crust.

3. Grill the chicken breast, and cut it into $\frac{1}{2}$-inch pieces. Set aside.

4. Sauté sliced mushrooms in a small amount of olive oil. Set aside.

5. Spread the pesto sauce evenly on the surface of the dough.

6. Top with mozzarella, covering the entire surface.

7. Top with chicken, onions, and mushrooms. Top with feta cheese.

8. Bake on preheated, greased cookie sheet until dough is brown and mozzarella cheese is melted, about 10–15 minutes.

YIELD: 2 SERVINGS AS A LIGHT ENTRÉE

# CHICKEN CORDON BLEU PIZZA

MAGIC CITY BREWERY,
BIRMINGHAM, AL

*If you happen to have access to a wood-fired brick oven, it makes a good bit of difference in the flavor of the pizza. It only takes three minutes to cook, as well. If you're pressed for time, use a commercially made pizza dough. Serve the pizza with a pale ale or oatmeal stout.*

1 6-ounce ball Pizza Dough (see recipe on page 40)

2 tablespoons Roasted Garlic Paste (see recipe at right)

1 6-ounce boneless and skinless chicken breast, grilled

$\frac{1}{4}$ pound ham, coarsely chopped

$\frac{1}{4}$ pound Swiss cheese, shredded

$\frac{1}{4}$ cup shredded mozzarella cheese

$\frac{1}{4}$ teaspoon dried oregano

1. Preheat oven to 450° F. Put a pizza stone or a greased cookie sheet in the oven.

2. On floured counter-top or board, roll Pizza Dough into an 8-inch circle using a rolling pin, or press out with the heels of both hands.

3. Using a spoon or rubber spatula, spread Roasted Garlic Paste over dough in an even layer, leaving about $\frac{1}{8}$ inch uncovered around the edge.

4. Top evenly with diced chicken and ham. Cover even-ly with cheeses, and sprinkle with oregano.

5. Cook on a dry, preheated pizza stone, lightly cov-ered with semolina flour, or on a greased preheated cookie sheet for 6–7 minutes, until cheese is melted and bubbly in the center.

## ROASTED GARLIC PASTE

1 bulb fresh whole garlic

3 tablespoons extra-virgin olive oil

1. Preheat oven to 350°F. Cut pointed end off a garlic bulb about ½ inch from end, exposing tips of garlic cloves within. Drizzle 1 tablespoon olive oil onto cut end of bulb.

2. Place garlic on cookie sheet on middle rack and bake for 45 minutes, or until garlic feels soft. Let cool for 20 minutes, and squeeze garlic out of cloves. It should be golden colored.

3. Place garlic in a food processor or blender, and turn unit on. Slowly drizzle 2 tablespoons of olive oil into the paste while the unit is on. This should take a full minute. Let blade turn for an additional minute to ensure that paste emulsifies.

# PIZZA DOUGH

(Makes 2 6-ounce dough balls)

$\frac{3}{4}$ cup warm water (100°F to 110°F)

1 tablespoon honey

1 package active dry yeast

1 tablespoon olive oil

1 teaspoon salt

2 cups high-gluten flour (such as bread flour)

1 tablespoon dried thyme

1. In a small bowl, combine water, honey, yeast, and olive oil, and mix well until yeast is completely suspended in liquid.

2. In a medium mixing bowl, stir together salt, flour, and thyme.

3. Slowly add liquid mixture to flour mixture, stirring with a spoon or fork. A relatively dry ball should form. If ball is sticky, add more flour, 1 teaspoon at a time, until you get a ball that can be worked with.

4. Place ball on floured surface, and knead for 4 minutes with the heels of your hand.

5. Place formed ball into lightly floured bowl, and cover bowl with a damp towel or plastic wrap. Let dough rise in a warm area of the kitchen for 1 hour.

6. Punch down dough and separate into 2 pieces.

YIELD: 1 8-INCH PIZZA (ENOUGH FOR ONE MEAL OR A SNACK FOR 2)

# CHAPTER 3
## SOUPS, CHILIS, AND STEWS

Cold weather induces hibernation in humans as it does in other mammals. Those of us who are lucky enough to have a fireplace know the pleasure of cuddling up and keeping warm. And nothing beats off the winter's chill like a hearty bowl of chili, soup, or stew.

Many brewpubs draw on regional ingredients for their stews and soups. For example, when Wanda Anderson makes her Green Chili Stew at Eske's in Taos, New Mexico, she uses freshly roasted green chilies. Others serve up variations on old family recipes, such as Ebbets Field's Nick Russo and his Italian Chicken Tortellini Soup.

With the exception of the most delicate soups, such as the Wheat Beer Potato Soup from Hops!, the combination of tastes in these one-pot meals will stand up to beers as hearty as bitters, stouts, and porters. These recipes were made with leftovers in mind, because the flavors will meld if the pot spends an extra day in the refrigerator.

# CRAB AND CORN CHOWDER

## CAPITOL CITY BREWING CO., WASHINGTON, DC

*Crab base is a concentrated flavoring used to make stock. It's available in many supermarkets and specialty food stores. This soup tastes best if made a day in advance and refrigerated, then reheated before serving. Serve it with a light-flavored beer, such as a wheat beer or light ale.*

$3\frac{1}{4}$ ounces bacon, diced

1 jumbo onion, peeled and diced

$\frac{1}{2}$ stalk celery, diced

$\frac{2}{3}$ pound crabmeat (claw)

$1\frac{1}{3}$ cups canned corn

1 medium-small potato, peeled and diced

$\frac{3}{4}$ cup crab base

$6\frac{1}{2}$ cups water

1 small jalapeño pepper, finely diced

$4\frac{1}{2}$–5 teaspoons Old Bay seasoning

$\frac{1}{4}$ teaspoon white pepper

$\frac{1}{4}$ cup butter

$\frac{1}{4}$ cup flour

$\frac{3}{4}$ cup diced roasted red peppers
(can use canned or pimientos)

$2\frac{1}{2}$ cups half-and-half

1. Sauté bacon in a large stockpot until almost crisp. Add onion and celery. Cook until onions are translucent.

2. Add crabmeat, corn, potato, crab base, water, jalapeño pepper, Old Bay seasoning, and white pepper. Bring to a boil.

3. Separately mix butter and flour thoroughly to make roux, add to soup to thicken.

4. Add roasted peppers and half-and-half.

YIELD: 4 QUARTS

# SMOKED SALMON CHOWDER

## ELM CITY BREWING CO., KEENE, NH

*Elm City makes its home in the Colony Mill Marketplace, a turn-of-the-century building that was formerly a toy factory. Elm City cold-smokes Pacific salmon and uses it in this chowder and in a salmon spread. It even sells smoked salmon to go from the restaurant. Cold-smoked salmon is also available, prepackaged, at seafood markets and many supermarkets. Elm City pairs this good, hearty soup with Lunch Pale Ale, a classic English-style pale ale.*

2 medium potatoes, peeled and cubed

2 stalks of celery, sliced

1 medium onion, diced

$1\frac{1}{2}$ cups clam juice

1 clove garlic, chopped

2 tablespoons chopped fresh parsley

$\frac{1}{4}$ cup butter

$\frac{1}{4}$ cup flour

$\frac{1}{2}$ pound cold-smoked Pacific salmon

1 cup light cream

$\frac{1}{2}$ cup milk

YIELD: 6-8 SERVINGS

1. In a soup kettle, simmer potatoes, celery, onion, and clam juice until vegetables are tender.

2. Add garlic and parsley.

3. Melt butter in a saucepan. Stir in flour and cook over low heat, stirring constantly. Add the roux into the vegetables, and simmer until thickened.

4. Add salmon, cream, and milk. Simmer another 10 minutes.

# ITALIAN CHICKEN TORTELLINI SOUP

## EBBETS FIELD, SPRINGFIELD, MO

*Proprietor Nick Russo suggests using additional chicken breasts if you want a heartier soup, and veggie lovers can add spinach. He adds, "dunking Italian bread into your soup is not only acceptable but also considered fashionable." This soup goes well with any full-bodied beer, such as an amber or bitter ale.*

2 large skinless chicken breasts

1 28-ounce can whole peeled tomatoes

2 large carrots, chopped

1–2 large stalks celery

6 large fresh basil leaves, chopped

$\frac{1}{2}$ clove fresh garlic, chopped

1 tablespoon pure olive oil

$\frac{1}{4}$ cup Chianti (red wine)

Salt and pepper to taste

1 12-ounce bag cheese-filled tortellini

Garnish: grated Romano cheese

1. Cook the chicken breasts in a pot containing $1\frac{1}{2}$ quarts of water over a low flame, until the chicken breasts are poached. Remove the chicken from the pot so it can cool. Strain the broth into a new pot.

2. Purée the tomatoes in a blender. Add the tomatoes to the chicken broth. Add the carrots, celery, basil, garlic, olive oil, Chianti, salt, and pepper. Cook until the carrots and celery are soft, about 1 hour.

3. Dice the chicken and add to the soup.

4. Cook the tortellini as directed on the package. Rinse the tortellini, and add to the soup. Add additional salt and pepper if needed. Top with a tablespoon of grated Romano cheese.

YIELD: 4–6 MAIN-COURSE SERVINGS

# BEER AND CHEESE SOUP

## MILL ROSE BREWING CO., SOUTH BARRINGTON, IL

*This makes a nice opener for a dinner, especially in the fall. Make it with a light ale. Many supermarkets carry chicken base, a concentrated, flavored soup base. A dark lager or other full-bodied beer, though nothing as full as a stout, will contrast nicely with the soup.*

$\frac{1}{2}$ cup finely diced green bell pepper

$\frac{1}{2}$ cup finely diced carrot

$\frac{1}{2}$ cup finely diced Spanish onion

$\frac{1}{2}$ cup finely diced celery

$\frac{1}{2}$ cup butter

1 scant cup flour

4 cups chicken stock

4 cups light ale or lager

2 tablespoons chicken base or bouillon

$\frac{1}{2}$ pound cheddar cheese, grated

$\frac{1}{4}$ pound blue cheese

$1\frac{1}{2}$ teaspoons cayenne pepper

1 teaspoon Worcestershire sauce

Salt to taste

1 teaspoon ground white pepper, or to taste

3 cups heavy cream

YIELD: $3\frac{1}{2}$–4 QUARTS

1. Sauté vegetables in the butter until soft but not browned. Add the flour and stir until it's smooth and forms a roux. Cook the mixture slowly until it foams.

2. Add the chicken stock, beer, and chicken base or bouillon to the vegetable mixture. Bring this to a boil, and allow to thicken. Strain the vegetables from the soup, and set them aside for later.

3. Return the soup to a medium heat, and simmer for about 20 minutes. Whisk in the cheeses, cayenne pepper, and Worcestershire. Season the soup with salt and white pepper to taste.

4. Add the heavy cream to the soup, and simmer quickly. Do not bring the soup to a boil after adding cream.

5. Add the reserved vegetable mixture, and check the seasoning.

# SEVEN ONION SOUP

## THE CHURCH BREW WORKS, PITTSBURGH, PA

*For those who have a religious devotion to good beer, this is the brewpub for you. It is located in a deconsecrated church that was built in 1902, and the brewhouse is set up in the former altar area. The walls are replete with stained-glass windows. Dunkel is a dark lager beer with a clean and roasty aroma. It works well both in and with this soup—the intensely reduced flavor of the dunkel in the soup pairs wonderfully with the crisp finish of the beer served alongside.*

$\frac{1}{4}$ cup butter

2 Spanish onions, chopped

1 red onion, chopped

1 Vidalia onion, chopped

1 leek, chopped

4 shallots, chopped

4 green onions, chopped

12 chives, chopped

1 tablespoon minced garlic

4 cups dunkel

4 cups chicken stock

2 cups beef stock

1 tablespoon sugar

Pinch of salt

Pinch of black pepper

$\frac{1}{2}$ teaspoon dried thyme

Garnish: croutons with provolone cheese melted on top

YIELD: 2 QUARTS, SERVING 8 AS AN APPETIZER

1. Melt the butter in a 1-gallon pot. Add Spanish onions, red onion, Vidalia onion, leek, shallots, and green onions. Sweat the six onions for approximately 5 minutes on low heat, until slightly browned.

2. Add the dunkel and cook until the liquid is reduced by half.

3. Add the chives, garlic, chicken stock, beef stock, sugar, salt, pepper, and thyme. Bring to a simmer for approximately 5 minutes or until the onions are soft.

# IRON HORSE STOUT CHILI

## BIG RIVER GRILLE AND BREWING WORKS, CHATTANOOGA, TN

*Great on a cold winter's day, Iron Horse Stout Chili was named after the beer Big River Grille uses in the recipe. It adds a robust flavor that carries throughout the taste experience. Enjoy this chili with a medium-bodied ale or perhaps a sweeter wheat or honey beer.*

2½ pounds ground beef

2 tablespoons minced garlic

1 cup stout

2 cups diced onion

1 cup diced green peppers

2 tablespoons diced jalapeños

¾ cup chili powder

2 tablespoons cumin

2 tablespoons salt

1 tablespoon cayenne pepper

Pinch of oregano leaves

48 ounces canned stewed tomatoes

24 ounces canned pinto beans, drained

24 ounces canned kidney beans, drained

24 ounces canned black beans, drained

**YIELD: 5 QUARTS**

1. In a skillet, braise the beef with garlic and beer. When beef is thoroughly cooked, remove from heat and drain. Place meat into another large pot.

2. In a saucepan, cook vegetables and spices until translucent, approximately 10 minutes. Add tomatoes and reduce heat to medium-low.

3. Bring mixture to a simmer, stirring frequently. Add mixture and beans to meat.

4. Bring all ingredients to a simmer, and serve.

# VEGETARIAN GREEN CHILI STEW

## ESKE'S BREW PUB & EATERY, TAOS, NM

*In northern New Mexico it seems every family has its own "secret ingredient" for green chili stew. The one constant in most traditional recipes is meat. However, Chef and co-owner Wanda Anderson leans toward a vegetarian diet, as do many of Eske's patrons, so she decided to change her family's recipe and switch the meat for squash. Anderson makes her green chili stew with freshly roasted, medium-heat, Hatch green chilies, but says frozen chilies will also work, or use canned. And if you prefer hot chili, then use hot! At the pub, the stew is served with whole wheat tortillas and an assertive, hoppy pale ale.*

1 cup diced yellow onion

3 cups quartered and sliced zucchini squash

1 cup diced yellow summer squash

1 medium carrot, thinly sliced

6 large cloves garlic

3 cups sliced mushrooms

1 tablespoon oregano

1 tablespoon ground cumin

2 tablespoons canola oil, plus 6 tablespoons canola oil or butter

$\frac{1}{2}$ cup flour

3 cups vegetable broth, cooled

$3\frac{1}{2}$ cups cold water

2 large potatoes, diced

$3\frac{1}{2}$ cups chopped green chilies

Salt and pepper to taste

Garnish: diced tomatoes, chopped onion, shredded mild cheddar cheese

1. Sauté onion, zucchini, yellow squash, carrot, garlic, mushrooms, oregano, and cumin in 2 tablespoons canola oil until vegetables are soft.

2. While they are cooking, start a roux with the flour and 6 tablespoons canola oil or butter, cooking until lightly browned.

3. Add vegetable broth, water, potatoes, green chilies, and the roux to the vegetables. Simmer until the potatoes are cooked and the stew has thickened. Add salt and pepper and stir often to keep the stew from sticking to the bottom of the pot. Garnish with tomatoes, chopped onion, and cheddar.

YIELD: 9 SERVINGS OF APPROXIMATELY
2 CUPS EACH

# JAMBALAYA WITH CREOLE SAUCE

## EMPIRE BREWING CO., SYRACUSE, NY

*This Cajun stew is the best-selling item at Empire, whose menu features Cajun food, Mexican cuisine, and more. An amber beer or a pale ale will complement the spiciness of this dish.*

½ cup chopped onion

½ cup chopped celery

2 cups whole peeled tomatoes, broken up slightly

½ cup chopped green pepper

1 clove garlic, minced

½ cup vegetable oil

½ pound andouille sausage
(or other spicy sausage), cut in ½-inch dice

1½ cups diced smoked ham

½ pound cooked crawfish tails (or substitute other seafood)

½ pound raw shrimp

2 cups raw rice

2 tablespoons fresh chopped parsley

⅓ cup chopped cilantro

4 cups chicken stock

¼ teaspoon cayenne pepper

1 teaspoon sugar

1 bay leaf

⅓ teaspoon black pepper

¼ teaspoon thyme

½ teaspoon oregano

Creole Sauce (see recipe at right)

1. In a heavy-bottomed pan, sauté the onion, celery, tomatoes, green pepper, and garlic in the oil until they are soft.

2. Add the sausage, ham, and seafood, and sauté for another 10 minutes.

3. Add the rice, and stir until all of the rice is coated with the oil.

4. Add the rest of the ingredients and cover. Bring to a boil. Simmer until almost all of the liquid is absorbed and the rice is tender. Remove bay leaf. Serve topped with Creole Sauce.

## CREOLE SAUCE

$\frac{1}{2}$ cup butter

$\frac{1}{2}$ cup diced onion

$\frac{1}{2}$ cup roughly chopped celery

2 cups chopped green pepper

2 tablespoons minced garlic

1 cup roughly chopped tomato

1 tablespoon sugar

3 cups chicken stock

1 teaspoon Tabasco sauce

$\frac{1}{2}$ bay leaf

1. Melt butter in a large skillet over medium heat.

2. Add onion, celery, green pepper, and garlic, and cook until soft.

3. Add tomato, sugar, stock, Tabasco, and bay leaf, and cook for 30 minutes.

4. Remove the bay leaf, and purée the warm sauce in a blender. (Be careful: Using the blender to purée warm things can be dangerous. Start out with a slow speed.)

**YIELD: APPROXIMATELY 3$\frac{1}{2}$ QUARTS**

# WHEAT BEER POTATO SOUP

## HOPS! BISTRO & BREWERY., SCOTTSDALE, AZ

*Hops!, one of a chain of brewpubs located in Arizona and California, is an elegant restaurant in an upscale shopping mall. Executive Chef Alan Skversky explains that the reason the hefeweiss is added last is because of the unfiltered yeast in this style of wheat beer. It will get bitter if exposed to a high amount of heat and cooked. Serve this soup with a wheat beer or a golden ale.*

2 pounds russet potatoes, peeled and diced large

$\frac{1}{2}$ pound onions, diced

$\frac{1}{2}$ pound carrots, diced

2 quarts chicken stock

2 cups heavy cream

2 cups hefeweiss

Salt and pepper to taste

Garnish: croutons, shredded cheddar cheese

1. Boil potatoes, onions, and carrots in chicken stock until soft. Blend well in a blender.

2. Reheat mixture, and add cream. Add beer and salt and pepper to taste. It is not necessary to strain.

3. Serve with croutons and shredded cheddar cheese.

YIELD: 8–10 SERVINGS

# CHAPTER 4

# SALADS AND PASTA DISHES

**M**any of us concerned with eating healthier food make the mistake of believing that this means sacrificing taste. But healthy food doesn't have to be that way. Adding grilled vegetables, seafood, or knockout dressings to a salad is one way to make what's good for you taste good, too.

While some of the pasta recipes here verge on the decadent, others show that you don't have to coat your linguine or capellini with a rich, heavy sauce to make it taste delicious. The use of fresh ingredients will provide all the flavor you could ask for.

Most of these salads and pastas have enough spiciness to stand up to beers in the middle of the spectrum—medium-bodied ales such as pale ales, or crisp lagers like pilsners. Although fruit beers traditionally don't match well with non-dessert items, a fruit beer can complement a dish served with a fruit-based relish, such as the Peach Salsa served with Eddie McStiff's Grilled Tuna Salad (p. 66).

# LINGUINE OASIS

## ITALIAN OASIS & BREWERY, LITTLETON, NH

*Serve this pasta dish accompanied by garlic bread. Italian Oasis owner Wayne Morello recommends pairing it with a pale ale, because the light, clean taste will complement rather than overwhelm the pasta.*

2 tablespoons unsalted butter

1 teaspoon fresh minced garlic

4–5 fresh broccoli florets

2 Spanish artichoke hearts, quartered

3 tablespoons chopped fresh tomato

2 tablespoons sliced black olives

Fresh oregano to taste

Fresh basil to taste

$\frac{1}{4}$ cup dry Italian white wine

$\frac{1}{4}$ pound linguine, cooked

1. Melt butter in medium saucepan at medium-high heat. Add garlic, and sauté for 30 seconds. Add broccoli and artichoke hearts, and cook 2–3 minutes. Add tomato, olives, oregano, and basil, and cook 1 minute. Add wine, and cook 1 minute more.

2. Add linguine and toss. Season with salt and pepper.

YIELD: 1 SERVING

# FETTUCCINE WITH WEISSBIER CREAM

## ZIP CITY BREWING CO., NEW YORK, NY

*Feel free to substitute any pasta with this sauce. It also works well with stuffed pastas such as ravioli and tortellini. While there's an ample amount of cream and butter in this dish, the richness is balanced by the wheat beer. Zip City recommends a hefeweiss or Märzen to drink with the pasta.*

1 pound uncooked fettuccine

$\frac{1}{2}$ cup butter

$1\frac{1}{3}$ tablespoons minced garlic

1 cup weissbier

1 pint heavy cream

$\frac{1}{8}$ teaspoon nutmeg

Salt to taste

Pepper to taste

1 tablespoon minced parsley

Grated Parmesan cheese

1. Cook fettuccine in boiling salted water until al dente (cooked, but still firm to the bite). Drain. While pasta is cooking, heat butter in sauté pan. Add garlic and weissbier. Reduce by half.

2. Add cream, and continue reducing the liquid until the sauce coats the back of a spoon. Season with nutmeg, salt, pepper, and parsley.

3. Add fettuccine to sauce. Heat through, tossing to coat the pasta evenly. Place pasta in 4 pasta bowls. Serve with grated Parmesan cheese.

**YIELD: 4 SERVINGS**

# CAESAR SALAD WITH FOCACCIA

## IL VICINO WOOD OVEN PIZZA & BREWERY, SALIDA, CO

*This brewpub, the original Il Vicino, uses a lot of garlic in its Caesar Salad. The hoppiness of an India Pale Ale will complement that. The recipe for Focaccia stands well on its own.*

### CAESAR SALAD

1 egg yolk

1 teaspoon Dijon mustard

Juice of $\frac{1}{2}$ fresh lemon

1 teaspoon puréed anchovy

1 teaspoon chopped garlic

Salt and pepper

$\frac{1}{2}$ cup extra-virgin olive oil

Croutons

1 ounce Parmesan cheese, coarsely grated

1 large handful of chopped romaine lettuce

Focaccia (see recipe at right)

Garnish: anchovies

1. In a stainless steel bowl, using a stainless steel whip, combine egg, mustard, lemon, anchovy, garlic, and a pinch of salt and pepper.

2. Slowly add olive oil to make a consistent mayonnaise.

3. Add croutons, Parmesan, and lettuce, and toss. The leaves of the lettuce should be evenly coated but not dripping.

4. Garnish with two whole anchovies, criss-crossed, and serve with a slice of fresh Focaccia.

## FOCACCIA

(Makes 1 loaf)

$\frac{1}{2}$ red onion, chopped

2 tablespoons rosemary

$2\frac{1}{2}$ cups warm water

2 tablespoons honey

2 tablespoons yeast

$\frac{1}{4}$ cup olive oil

8 cups flour

1 teaspoon salt

$\frac{1}{4}$ cup grated Parmesan cheese

1. Sauté onions and rosemary in olive oil until onions are translucent. Set aside.

2. Mix water, honey, and yeast, and wait a few minutes for yeast to react. Add olive oil, then slowly add flour and salt. Next add onion mixture. Knead for 12 minutes. (It's best to use a mixer, rather than doing it by hand.)

3. Lightly flour a cookie sheet. Roll out dough onto the cookie sheet until it is flat and even in thickness. Let dough rise for 30 minutes.

4. Preheat oven to 350° F. Spread more olive oil on the surface and poke it into the dough with your fingers to make it look like the surface of the moon. Sprinkle the cheese on top. Bake for 30 minutes, until it has a nice golden top.

YIELD: 1 LARGE SALAD, SERVING 1 AS A MEAL OR 2 AS AN APPETIZER

# GRILLED VEGETABLE SALAD WITH SESAME-GINGER VINAIGRETTE

## COPPERTANK BREWING CO., AUSTIN, TX

*This salad gives you another reason to fire up the grill on a Saturday afternoon. You can also broil the vegetables in your oven broiler. Mixed baby greens are commonly available in most produce sections of grocery stores. The mix usually contains such leaves as arugula, radicchio, endive, red oak, and several others. You can buy focaccia or make your own (see Il Vicino's on page 63). For more of a meal, add slices of smoked cheese such as Gouda, a grilled chicken breast, or beef tenderloin, using the vinaigrette as a marinade. Coppertank recommends pairing the salad with a hoppy pale ale or a traditional pilsner.*

1 green bell pepper

1 red bell pepper

1 large tomato, sliced thick

1 large red onion, cut into wedges

1 large Portobello mushroom

1 ear corn on the cob

1 loaf focaccia

$\frac{3}{4}$ pound mixed baby greens

Sesame-Ginger Vinaigrette (see recipe at right)

1. Lightly oil the peppers and place on the grill. Grill until the skin blisters, turning frequently to avoid burning. When completely blistered, place them in a bowl and cover with plastic wrap. After the peppers cool, scrape off the skins, remove the seeds, and cut into strips.

2. Lightly oil the tomato, onion, mushroom, and corn, and grill them, watching closely to avoid burning. Once grilled, cut the corn from the cob, the tomatoes into small sections, and the mushroom into thick slices.

3. Cut the focaccia into thick strips and grill slightly until brown and crisp.

4. Toss the baby greens with the vegetables and enough vinaigrette to coat lightly. Place on oversized plates, add strips of focaccia, and serve immediately.

## SESAME-GINGER VINAIGRETTE

2 tablespoons sesame seeds

$\frac{1}{4}$ cup rice vinegar

$\frac{1}{4}$ cup red wine vinegar

2 tablespoons minced fresh ginger root

1 tablespoon minced garlic

1 tablespoon minced onion

3 tablespoons teriyaki sauce

1 cup Sterling or other high-quality salad oil

2 teaspoons salt

2 teaspoons black pepper

1 teaspoon crushed red pepper flakes

1. Toss the sesame seeds in a pan over the fire until lightly browned. Place in a mixing bowl, and add the vinegars, ginger, garlic, onion, and teriyaki sauce.

2. Gradually whisk in the oil until smooth and completely incorporated. Season with the salt, pepper, and red pepper flakes. To enhance the flavor, warm the dressing in a pot on the grill while grilling the vegetables.

**YIELD: 4 SERVINGS**

# GRILLED TUNA SALAD WITH CORN RELISH AND PEACH SALSA

## EDDIE MCSTIFF'S RESTAURANT AND MICRO BREWERY, MOAB, UT

*This is one of the brewpub's most popular specials. The dish with a Southwestern flair is also very healthful for you. Note that you need to make the Peach Salsa at least four hours in advance of serving time. Eddie McStiff's recommends its Raspberry Wheat or Lime Ale, both of which are bottled, or any light-tasting beer with this dish.*

8 cups mixed greens
4 medium-sized, fresh tuna fillets

### PEACH SALSA

1 teaspoon salt

1 teaspoon pepper

8 fresh peaches, diced

1 jalapeño pepper, minced

Juice of 1 lime

1 red bell pepper, diced

1 red onion, diced

$\frac{1}{4}$ cup raspberry vinegar

YIELD: 4 SERVINGS

# CORN RELISH

4 cups corn kernels

1 cup canned black beans, drained

1 teaspoon salt

1 teaspoon pepper

1 teaspoon paprika

½ cup diced red bell pepper

1. Make Peach Salsa: Combine all ingredients. Refrigerate for 4 hours.

2. Make Corn Relish: In a large skillet, warm the corn kernels, and add remaining ingredients. Cook until relish is warm.

3. Divide mixed greens among 4 plates. Top each with 1 cup of Corn Relish.

4. Grill tuna fillets, and cut each into 4 or 5 strips. Place strips of grilled tuna atop the beds of Corn Relish.

5. Top each tuna fillet with 1 cup of Peach Salsa. Your favorite salad dressing can be offered on the side.

EDDIE McSTIFF'S

# "SONOMA" SHRIMP WITH CAPELLINI PASTA

## RICHBRAU BREWING CO. AND RESTAURANT, RICHMOND, VA

*Chef Matthew Tlusty created this dish while working in a small restaurant in Greenwich, Connecticut. "Each restaurant that I've worked in, I've brought this dish with me, and it has always been the biggest seller," he says. "When asked to create a restaurant in a brewery, where burgers and sandwiches were the biggest seller, I needed to come up with a dish that would dismiss the 'burger' atmosphere, bring me loyal followers, and go well with the beers we served." The brewpub serves it with its Golden Griffin Pale Ale, and any pale ale will match well with it.*

1 cup plus 1 tablespoon olive oil

½ cup garlic cloves, peeled

½ cup sun-dried tomatoes

1 pound shrimp (medium size; Black Tiger preferred)

½ cup chopped spinach

1½ cups white wine, plus more to soak tomatoes

1 cup unsalted butter

2 pounds capellini/angel hair pasta, cooked

**YIELD: 4 SERVINGS**

1. Caramelize garlic: Place 1 cup olive oil into a saucepan and heat over medium-high heat. Slowly add peeled garlic cloves to the oil, and simmer for 5 minutes. Lower the heat, and cook the garlic until browned. Finished garlic should be soft, like butter. Set aside.

2. Place the sun-dried tomatoes into a bowl of warm white wine, just enough to cover, and rehydrate until soft. Chop tomatoes into a fine dice.

3. In a large sauté pan, bring 1 tablespoon olive oil to the smoking point. Add the shrimp, and sauté until shrimp are done. While pan is still hot, add caramelized garlic and sun-dried tomatoes. Sauté for 1 minute, then add 1½ cups white wine. Let the wine reduce by half, and add a pinch of salt and pepper. Add the chopped spinach and butter. Keep stirring until the butter has melted.

4. Remove the shrimp from the pan, and add the pasta, reheating until hot. Serve shrimp over cooked pasta.

# PENNE PASTA

## UNION STATION BREWING CO., PROVIDENCE, RI

*Walls, a chimney, and other parts of Providence's old rail-road station are incorporated into the decor at Union Station. Tasso is a very spicy, intensely smoked Cajun ham. There is really nothing else like it, but if you can't find it, substitute another spicy smoked ham. Liaison is a mixture of heavy cream and egg yolks—for one egg yolk add one-and-a-third cups cream. The brewpub serves a West Coast-style pale ale with this dish.*

$\frac{1}{4}$ cup cooking oil

8 1-inch pieces of chicken

(Union Station uses chicken tenders)

2 tablespoons sliced mushrooms

2 tablespoons chopped tasso or other smoked ham

($\frac{1}{4}$-inch pieces)

1 teaspoon minced garlic

2 tablespoons white wine

$\frac{3}{4}$ cup liaison

2 tablespoons grated Parmesan cheese

1 teaspoon unsalted butter

2 tablespoons cooked peas

1 tablespoon chopped green onions

9 ounces cooked penne pasta

1. Heat a sauté pan. Place cooking oil in pan. Add diced chicken, and season with salt and pepper. Sear the chunks of chicken.

2. Add sliced mushrooms, tasso, and garlic. Sauté the mushrooms, and allow the spices from the tasso to cover the other ingredients in the pan.

3. Add white wine, and reduce until the wine dissipates.

4. Add liaison, Parmesan, butter, peas, and green onions. Allow the liaison to reduce into a thick, rich sauce, stirring constantly (about 2–3 minutes over high heat).

5. Once the sauce has formed, add the pasta, and mix. When the pasta is hot and completely coated with the rich cream sauce, the dish is ready to eat.

YIELD: 1 SERVING

# SPICY ANGEL HAIR PASTA

## RAGTIME TAVERN & GRILL, ATLANTIC BEACH, FL

*This dish is quick to prepare. The spicy seasonings will go nicely with a malty or hoppy red ale.*

¼ cup vegetable oil–olive oil blend
1 ounce garlic, minced
¼ pound poblano peppers, seeded and sliced
¼ pound red bell peppers, seeded and sliced
1 pint heavy cream
2 tablespoons Chili-Angel Seasoning
(see recipe below)
Juice of ½ lemon
1 ounce cilantro, stems removed, chopped
¼ cup chicken consommé or broth
1¼ pounds dried angel hair pasta

## CHILI-ANGEL SEASONING
¼ cup granulated garlic
2 tablespoons ground cumin
2 tablespoons chili powder

1. Heat oil over medium heat. Sauté garlic, poblano, and red pepper in oil. Add cream and reduce. Add seasoning, lemon juice, cilantro, and consommé or broth. Cook until thickened to desired consistency.

2. Cook pasta in boiling water until al dente. Drain. Toss sauce with pasta.

**YIELD: 4 SERVINGS**

# CHAPTER 5
# SEAFOOD ENTRÉES

Seafood is remarkably versatile in terms of preparation. You can steam it, poach it, fry or grill it, add spices or beer to it, top it with flavorful sauces or butters. The one thing you don't want to do, however, is overcook it. Remember, fish and shellfish require very little cooking time; if they are overcooked, they turn dry or rubbery.

While more subtly flavored fish can best be enjoyed with a light ale or lager, these dishes have enough "oomph" to take on bigger beers, including medium-bodied lagers and British-style ales. Hoppy beers work very well with fried fish, such as Broad Ripple's Fish and Chips (p. 75), because the hoppiness cuts right through any residual greasiness.

# SPICY BEER SHRIMP

## MILL STREET BREWING CO., ST. PAUL, MN

*Mill Street serves Spicy Beer Shrimp with a lemon crown, foc-cacia bread (see Il Vicino's on page 63), and a pint of pale ale.*

2 tablespoons olive oil

$\frac{1}{2}$ cup diced onion

$\frac{1}{4}$ cup minced garlic

2 pints American-style pale ale

$1\frac{1}{4}$ tablespoons chili powder

1 teaspoon cayenne pepper

$1\frac{1}{4}$ tablespoons crushed red pepper

$3\frac{1}{4}$ tablespoons chopped fresh parsley

1 pound shrimp, peeled and deveined

Garnish: lemon crowns, foccacia bread

1. Heat oil in pot. Add onion, and sauté until translucent. Add garlic, and cook 2 more minutes.

2. Add beer, chili powder, cayenne, red pepper, and parsley, and simmer for 15 minutes. Strain. Add shrimp to broth, and simmer for 3 minutes.

3. Divide into 4 equal portions, and serve with lemon crowns, foccacia bread, and a pint of pale ale.

YIELD: 1–2 SERVINGS AS A MAIN COURSE, OR 4 AS AN APPETIZER

# FISH AND CHIPS

## BROAD RIPPLE BREWPUB, INDIANAPOLIS, IN

*What pub would be complete without fish and chips? This is a hot seller at the brewpub. You can use any kind of English-style ale in the fish batter, even a stout. Serve fish and chips with a pale ale.*

4–5 pounds cod fillets, cut into 3- to 5-ounce portions
Flour
Beer Batter (see recipe below)
Vegetable oil for frying
Chips or french fries
Garnish: tartar sauce, malt vinegar (optional)

1. Roll cod pieces in flour, and submerge in Beer Batter.

2. Heat oil in fryer or deep frying pan. Cook fish until golden brown. Serve with chips or french fries, tartar sauce, and malt vinegar.

## BEER BATTER

2 cups flour
3 teaspoons paprika
3 tablespoons seasoning salt
2 teaspoons white pepper
3 tablespoons dried onions
$1\frac{1}{2}$ cups beer

1. Combine all ingredients, stirring until smooth. Add more beer if mixture seems too thick.

**YIELD: 10 SERVINGS**

# BRAISED HALIBUT WITH VEGETABLES AND HERBS

## PYRAMID ALEHOUSE & THOMAS KEMPER BREWERY, SEATTLE, WA

*This dish was created as a simple yet flavorful way to enhance the character of fresh halibut with a spicy blend of vegetables and the crisp, refreshing character of an American-style wheat beer. Serve with garlic mashed potatoes and either the same beer or a Belgian-style "white beer," such as Thomas Kemper's Belgian White.*

3 tablespoons peeled and diced celery

3 tablespoons peeled and diced carrots

3 tablespoons diced red onion

$\frac{1}{4}$ teaspoon minced garlic

2 bay leaves

1 teaspoon fresh thyme

$\frac{1}{4}$ teaspoon black pepper

3 tablespoons unsalted butter

1 cup Thomas Kemper Hefeweizen, or other wheat beer

1 cup fish or chicken stock

$\frac{1}{4}$ teaspoon curry powder

Pinch white sugar

2 tablespoons chopped Italian parsley

4 halibut fillets or steaks, 6–7 ounces each

Garnish: chopped parsley

1. Put all the ingredients except halibut into a large shallow pan, and bring to a boil. Boil for 1 minute.

2. Add the halibut fillets, cover, and turn down the heat to low. Simmer for about 8 minutes, or until halibut is cooked through. (Fish will feel firm to the touch when pressed.)

3. Remove fish to a serving platter or plates, and pour remaining broth over halibut portions. Garnish with chopped parsley.

YIELD: 4 SERVINGS

# HARVEST AMBER
# ALE BBQ SHRIMP

## FLATLANDER'S CHOPHOUSE & BREWERY,
## LINCOLNSHIRE, IL

*Flatlander's prepares this dish with its Harvest Amber Ale, a moderately hoppy amber, and serves it with wild rice and sauerkraut (see Federal Jack's on page 33). A hoppy pale ale provides a nice contrast, or you can complement the shrimp with the same amber ale you used to prepare it.*

2 tablespoons olive oil

1 cup amber ale

1 pound shrimp, 16–20 count, peeled and cleaned

1 cup Amber Ale BBQ Sauce (see recipe at right)

1 cup sauerkraut

1 cup cooked wild rice

Garnish: $\frac{1}{2}$ cup chopped green onions

1. Heat oil and beer in sauté pan. Add shrimp, and sauté until tender.

2. Add Amber Ale BBQ Sauce to pan, and toss until well blended.

3. To serve: Place $\frac{1}{2}$ cup wild rice and $\frac{1}{2}$ cup sauerkraut on center of each plate. Place cooked shrimp around the rice and sauerkraut. Pour excess sauce over the shrimp. Garnish with chopped green onions.

## AMBER ALE BBQ SAUCE

½ cup amber ale
1 tablespoon granulated garlic
1 tablespoon white pepper
1 quart Cattlemen's Classic BBQ sauce, or your favorite
barbecue sauce

1. In a mixing container, combine amber ale, garlic, and white pepper. Mix until smooth.

2. Add barbecue sauce, and stir with a wire whisk until well-blended.

3. Heat sauce to 160°F before serving.

**YIELD: 2 SERVINGS**

# DOCK STREET BEER SEAFOOD FEST

## DOCK STREET BREWING CO., PHILADELPHIA, PA

*All in one dish, the best accompaniments with beer: pota-toes, shellfish, fatty fish, meaty fish, spice, and asparagus. A delicate, simple, interesting and flavorful natural dish. Dock Street bottled beers are available in many states. Serve this fish dish with Dock Street Bohemian or any other pilsner.*

4 russet potatoes, peeled and cut in ovals

1 pound asparagus tips

$\frac{3}{4}$ pound seabass fillet, skin on (or any kind of bass)

$\frac{3}{4}$ pound salmon fillet, skin on

Salt and pepper

6 tablespoons cold butter, plus butter to coat pan

8 oysters in the shell, brushed and cleaned

1 12-ounce bottle Dock Street Bohemian Pilsner, or other pilsner

$\frac{1}{4}$ teaspoon caraway seeds

$\frac{1}{2}$ pound mussels, cleaned

Garnish: 2 tablespoons chopped parsley

1. Cook the potatoes thoroughly in salted water.

2. Cook the asparagus in salted water until al dente, then refresh in ice water.

3. Cut each fish fillet into 4 slices, and season with salt and pepper.

4. Butter the bottom of a large saucepan. Add the fish pieces and the oysters, and pour the beer and caraway seeds on top.

5. Bring to a boil, cover, and reduce the heat. After 2 minutes, add the potatoes and mussels. Cover and let simmer until the mussels open.

6. Remove the fish, shellfish, and potatoes to a deep plate. Bring the remaining liquid to a boil. With a whisk, gently introduce the 6 tablespoons cold butter into the liquid, a little at a time. Turn the flame on and off or move the pan on and off of the burner to keep the butter from breaking.

7. Add the asparagus to the liquid, and pour over the seafood. Sprinkle with fresh parsley.

YIELD: 4 SERVINGS

# PUMPKIN-SPICED SALMON

## BOSTON BEER WORKS, BOSTON, MA

*Located in the shadow of Fenway Park, Boston Beer Works draws crowds for its food and award-winning beers even when the Red Sox aren't in town. Arrowroot is a thickening agent that gives sauces a more delicate texture than cornstarch or flour. It's available in most supermarkets and specialty food stores. Boston Beer Works uses its Pumpkinhead Ale, a pumpkin-flavored beer, in this dish. The richness of the salmon will bring out the malty flavors of a Märzen or Oktoberfest beer.*

2 quarts pumpkin ale

1 cup honey

$\frac{1}{2}$ cup brown sugar

1 tablespoon cumin

$\frac{1}{4}$ cup pumpkin pie spice

$1\frac{1}{2}$ teaspoons cinnamon

$\frac{1}{2}$ cup crushed pumpkin seeds

1 cup orange juice

$\frac{1}{4}$ cup arrowroot (can substitute $\frac{5}{8}$ cup flour
or 5 tablespoons cornstarch)

1 10-ounce Atlantic salmon fillet

Vegetable oil

Salt and pepper

Garnish: toasted pumpkin seeds

YIELD: 2 SERVINGS

1. Prepare Pumpkin Glaze: In large pot over medium heat, combine ale, honey, brown sugar, cumin, pumpkin pie spice, cinnamon, and crushed pumpkin seeds. Reduce by half.

2. Combine orange juice and arrowroot until smooth. Stir into Pumpkin Glaze mixture, and continue cooking until thickened.

3. Brush salmon fillet with oil, and sprinkle with salt and pepper. Grill 3 minutes on each side for medium rare (still pink in the middle). Baste with Pumpkin Glaze while cooking.

4. Serve with additional Pumpkin Glaze and toasted pumpkin seeds.

# CARIBBEAN MANGO TUNA

## OLDE TOWNE TAVERN & BREWING CO., GAITHERSBURG, MD

*This tuna is a summer favorite at the brewpub. It may be cooked on an outdoor grill or in the oven. Feel free to marinate the tuna overnight in your favorite liquid, but avoid sweet marinades. The sweet flavor should be reserved for the salsa, which will soften the spicy flavor of the black beans and tuna. Note that you'll need to soak the beans for the Black Bean Sauce overnight. The Olde Towne Tavern serves this dish accompanied by red beans and rice or fried potatoes. Pair it with a porter or other full-flavored beer.*

Ground red pepper

Black pepper

White pepper

Cinnamon

4 tuna steaks

Black Bean Sauce (see recipe at right)

Mango and Papaya Salsa (see recipe at right)

1. Prepare Pepper Mixture: Combine red pepper, black pepper, white pepper, and cinnamon, adjusting seasonings to your taste. You will need additional Pepper Mixture for the Black Bean Sauce.

2. Lightly coat tuna steaks with Pepper Mixture. Grill on a flat surface or barbecue grill until medium-well to well-done. Leaving the fish slightly undercooked will retain natural moisture and flavor.

3. To serve: After grilling tuna, pour a line of Black Bean Sauce at the bottom of each plate. Place tuna on top of sauce, and top with a generous portion of Mango and Papaya Salsa.

## BLACK BEAN SAUCE

2 cups dried black beans
4 cups water, plus more if needed
Pepper Mixture
Fish bouillon or smoked ham hock, or similar
smoked or cured pig body part

1. Wash beans and soak in water overnight. Add water if necessary to fill to twice the height of the beans.

2. Boil beans with fish bouillon or pig part until soft. Add Pepper Mixture to taste.

3. Purée half the beans. Return to pot, and simmer with remaining beans. Mixture should be of a lumpy sauce consistency. Remove water if necessary, or simmer it off.

## MANGO AND PAPAYA SALSA

1 large papaya, cleaned and diced
1 large mango, cleaned and diced
1 tomato, cleaned and diced
1 green pepper, cleaned and diced
$\frac{1}{2}$ bunch fresh cilantro, chopped fine
Juice of 2 limes

1. Combine all ingredients.

YIELD: 4 SERVINGS

# SPICY BEER-STEAMED MUSSELS WITH ANCHO BUTTER

## GRIZZLY PEAK BREWING CO., ANN ARBOR, MI

*To caramelize the onion for the Spicy Beer Broth, cook it in a small amount of butter over low heat until brown. Lobster and clam base are intensely flavored soup seasonings, available in many supermarkets and specialty food stores. You can use any kind of beer (except a flavored beer such as a fruit beer) to cook the sausage. Serve the mussels with something full-bodied and aggressive, such as a stout.*

6 ounces Cajun sausage

Beer to cover sausage

$\frac{1}{4}$ cup olive oil

1 pound fresh mussels, rinsed and de-bearded

$1\frac{1}{2}$ cups Spicy Beer Broth (see recipe at right)

Garnish: $1\frac{1}{2}$ teaspoons chopped fresh parsley, 1 tablespoon Ancho Butter (see recipe on page 88)

1. Boil Cajun sausage in enough beer to cover until cooked through (how long will depend on the thickness of the sausage). Remove sausage from beer and grill just long enough to char it on the outside. Chill, and cut into 1-inch pieces.

2. Heat oil in sauté pan. Add sausage and cook 1–2 minutes. Add mussels, and sauté until shells just begin to open. Add Spicy Beer Broth, and cook over medium heat 4–5 minutes, until broth is hot.

3. Serve in a large bowl, garnished with chopped parsley and Ancho Butter.

## SPICY BEER BROTH

(Makes 2 quarts)

1 small yellow onion, sliced thin and caramelized

$\frac{1}{4}$ pound whole garlic cloves, peeled, roasted, and roughly chopped

$\frac{1}{2}$ ounce lobster base

$1\frac{1}{2}$ cups water

2 cups finely chopped Roma tomatoes

2 cups porter, or other dark ale

$\frac{1}{2}$ teaspoon salt

$\frac{1}{8}$ teaspoon cayenne pepper

1 tablespoon Worcestershire sauce

$\frac{1}{4}$ ounce clam base

$\frac{1}{2}$ cup chopped fresh parsley

$1\frac{1}{2}$ teaspoons minced chipotle peppers

1. Combine all ingredients in a saucepan. Bring to a boil, then reduce to a simmer and cook for 15 minutes.

# ANCHO BUTTER

$\frac{1}{2}$ pound unsalted butter

2 dried ancho chilies

2 cloves fresh garlic, peeled and minced

$\frac{1}{8}$ teaspoon Tabasco sauce

$\frac{1}{8}$ teaspoon salt

$\frac{1}{8}$ teaspoon cayenne pepper

$1\frac{1}{2}$ teaspoons finely chopped fresh cilantro

$1\frac{1}{2}$ teaspoons finely chopped fresh parsley

2 teaspoons lemon juice

1. Allow butter to warm to room temperature.

2. Broil ancho chilies until lightly toasted. Remove from heat, and soak in warm water until they soften. Remove seeds and stems from chilies, mince, and mash into a paste.

3. Combine all ingredients in a mixing bowl and blend well. Roll butter into 2-inch logs and freeze, wrapped in plastic wrap. To use, remove wrap and cut into coins.

YIELD: 1–2 SERVINGS AS A MAIN DISH,
2–4 AS AN APPETIZER

# CHAPTER 6

# POULTRY ENTRÉES

C hicken is extremely versatile and easy to prepare, and it responds well to many kinds of seasonings. In the following recipes, you'll find chicken with Indian spices, chicken enhanced by cheese, Southwestern-style chicken, chicken in a pie, and of course, chicken cooked in beer.

The beers selected to go with these entrées run from light wheat beers to medium-bodied ales. Beers made with roasted malts, such as porters and stouts, may detract too much from the spices and seasonings.

# DEEP ENDERS CHICKEN

## BUCKHORN SALOON AT ANDERSON VALLEY BREWING CO., BOONVILLE, CA

*This quick and simple summertime meal requires very little work for a wonderful taste. It's best if prepared on a barbecue grill. Serve the chicken with rice or baked potatoes. Anderson Valley's beers are available nationwide. Accompany the dish with the brewery's Boont Amber Ale or another amber ale.*

Salt and freshly ground pepper
2½-3 pounds boneless chicken thighs
1 22-ounce bottle Deep Enders Dark Porter,
or another porter

1. Rub chicken with salt and pepper. Place in shallow dish. Add beer and marinate for at least 2 hours or overnight in refrigerator.

2. Remove chicken from beer, reserving beer. Barbecue until done, or bake at 350°F for 30–40 minutes. Baste with reserved beer 2 or 3 times while cooking.

YIELD: 4 SERVINGS

# BREWHOUSE CHICKEN ALFREDO

## RANDY'S FUNHUNTERS BREWERY, WHITEWATER, WI

*You can make your own Alfredo sauce or buy it from the supermarket. Serve this chicken dish over fettuccine. A pale ale will go great with this entrée.*

4 7-ounce boneless chicken breasts
Oil for sautéing
2 shallots, finely chopped
1 cup fresh mushrooms, sliced
3 cups Alfredo sauce
$\frac{1}{2}$ cup oatmeal stout
2 tablespoons gin
2 pounds cooked fettuccine

1. Sauté chicken breasts for 3 minutes in a little oil. Turn chicken over, and add shallots and mushrooms. Cook for 3 minutes more.

2. Add gin, heating to burn off the alcohol. Remove chicken from the pan, and add Alfredo sauce and oatmeal stout to pan. Bring to a boil and simmer.

3. Add chicken, and cook until it is hot. Serve over cooked fettuccine.

YIELD: 4 SERVINGS

# BRAISED CHICKEN IN WEIZEN ALE

## OZARK BREWING CO., FAYETTEVILLE, AR

*This is a great recipe for a cold winter night. The hearty vegetables and flavorful chicken quickly give comfort to tired and weary bodies. You can use beer other than weizen with this dish, but stay away from any of the heavily hopped varieties or the darker beers such as stouts. A hefeweizen is best because of the smooth flavor and lemon tang it brings to the dish. Accompany it with a light-style ale or lager.*

1 2¼-pound whole chicken
Cooking twine
4 cloves fresh garlic
2 tablespoons salt
2 tablespoons black pepper
1 medium yellow onion
1 quart weizen (weissbier)
2 sprigs fresh rosemary
2 pounds small new potatoes
1 pound carrots, julienned
1 pound acorn squash, peeled, seeded
and cut into chunks

1. Preheat oven to 450°F. Wash the inside of the chicken under cold water, and pat dry. Season the cavity with the garlic, salt, and pepper. Add the onion, and close the cavity with the cooking twine.

2. Place chicken in a roasting pan in the oven for 15 minutes, then reduce heat to 325°F.

3. Add the weizen, rosemary, potatoes, carrots, and squash to the roasting pan. Continue basting the chicken occasionally with the beer for another 45–60 minutes.

4. Remove chicken from oven, and allow to cool for 15 minutes before carving and serving.

5. At this point, you can strain out the vegetables and serve separately, or serve them in the broth. If you serve separately, you may want to thicken the sauce with a small amount of roux (butter and flour) and sour cream.

YIELD: 2–4 SERVINGS

# SANTA FE CHICKEN

## NORTH COAST BREWING CO., FORT BRAGG, CA

*This chicken dish is one of North Coast's year-round best sellers. The brewpub garnishes it with fresh salsa and serves it with black beans and rice. Chorizo, a Mexican sausage, and chipotle peppers in adobo sauce are available in many supermarkets and specialty food stores. Accompany this dish with a nice, hoppy pale ale, such as North Coast's widely distributed Red Seal Ale.*

6 whole, boneless, skinless chicken breasts,
about 7 ounces each
1 small yellow onion, julienned
1 small green bell pepper, julienned
1 small red bell pepper, julienned
1 tablespoon chopped garlic
1 tablespoon brandy
1 pound chorizo sausage
$\frac{1}{2}$ pound hot pepper jack cheese, grated
2 eggs, beaten
1 cup milk
Flour as needed
Chipotle Sauce (see recipe at right)

1. Flatten chicken between pieces of wax paper with meat mallet. Set aside.

2. In medium sauté pan, sauté onion, green pepper, and red pepper over medium-high heat about 3–4 minutes, until they start to soften. Add garlic and stir.

3. Remove from heat. Flambé with brandy: Pour brandy over vegetables and light with a match. When flames subside, set mixture aside to cool in a separate bowl.

4. In the same pan, sauté chorizo until cooked through. Cool.

5. Mix the pepper mixture and chorizo together. Add the hot pepper jack cheese, and mix. Form into six $2\frac{1}{2}$–3-ounce ovals. Place 1 oval in center of each flattened chicken breast and fold into a round. Chill in freezer for 30 minutes.

6. Preheat oven to 350°F. Remove chicken rounds from freezer and dip into mixture of beaten eggs and milk, then coat with flour. Deep fry or sauté 4–5 minutes. Remove from fryer or sauté pan, and place on a deep baking sheet. Bake chicken for 15 minutes.

7. While chicken is baking, prepare Chipotle Sauce. Pour over baked chicken and serve.

## CHIPOTLE SAUCE

(Makes $1\frac{1}{2}$ cups)
1–2 chipotle peppers in adobo sauce
$\frac{1}{2}$ cup white wine
1 cup heavy cream
Salt and pepper to taste

1. Purée peppers in blender or food processor.

2. Pour wine into sauté pan, and add chipotle peppers; reduce by half. Add cream.

3. Cook over medium heat until thickened. Add salt and pepper to taste.

YIELD: 6 SERVINGS

# COCK-A-LEEKIE PIE

## THE VERMONT PUB & BREWERY, BURLINGTON, VT

*This recipe has a quaint and ancient history. When the widowed Mary Queen of Scots left France to claim the Scottish throne in 1561, she brought her cooks along with her. One of the dishes the kitchen produced was Coq au Leek. With time and Scots dialect, Coq au Leek became Cock-A-Leekie. Classic Cock-A-Leekie is a soup, but the Vermont Pub has transformed it into a savory pie. Serve it with a malty, hoppy ale.*

1⅔ pounds potatoes, sliced ¼-inch thick

1 cup ¼-inch-dice celery

1 cup ¼-inch-dice carrots

1 tablespoon unsalted butter

5½ cups chicken broth, preferably homemade

1 teaspoon soy sauce

½ teaspoon Worcestershire sauce

Flour and Spice Mix (see recipe at right)

1½ pounds boneless, skinless chicken breast, cut in ½-inch dice

⅔ cup heavy cream

⅔ cup raisins

Frozen puff pastry sheets

1. Boil the sliced potatoes in a large pot until barely cooked. Drain well in a colander; set aside.

2. In a large saucepan, sauté the carrots and celery in butter until translucent.

3. Add the cooked potato, chicken broth, soy sauce, and Worcestershire sauce to the vegetables in the pot. Bring to a simmer.

4. Combine Flour and Spice Mix in a large bowl with the chicken, coating the chicken well. Add the coated chicken to the simmering pot. Do not stir, just push the chicken below the level of the liquid. Simmer on medium heat for 20 minutes.

5. Reduce heat to low, and add the heavy cream and raisins. Simmer 20 more minutes, stirring occasionally. Correct seasoning to taste.

6. Distribute the chicken filling evenly into 6 small ovenproof casseroles or soup bowls. Cut puff pastry sheets to fit over the top of the casseroles or bowls. Bake as instructed on the puff pastry package.

## FLOUR AND SPICE MIX

1 cup all-purpose flour

$\frac{1}{4}$ teaspoon salt

$\frac{1}{4}$ teaspoon ground black pepper

$\frac{1}{2}$ teaspoon finely minced garlic

$\frac{1}{2}$ teaspoon onion powder

$\frac{1}{4}$ teaspoon sage

1. Combine all ingredients. Mix well.

**YIELD: 6 GENEROUS SERVINGS**

# ANASAZI CHICKEN

## COTTONWOOD GRILLE & BREWERY, BOONE, NC

*Goat cheese, ancho chilies, "tobacco" onions, and a rich, robust Madeira wine sauce artfully combine to make this recipe a Southwestern original. You can buy demi-glace mix at a supermarket or specialty food store—Knorr's is one brand. Purchase dried and de-seeded ancho chilies. Cottonwood serves Anasazi Chicken with saffron rice and black beans. It goes well with an amber ale.*

2 medium-sized red onions

Milk to cover onions

1 cup flour

Dash cayenne pepper

Dash ground cumin

Dash garlic powder

$\frac{1}{4}$ cup paprika

Dash onion powder

Dash salt

4 dried, deseeded ancho chilies

6 cups water

$\frac{1}{2}$ cup demi-glace

10 ounces goat cheese

$\frac{1}{4}$ cup grated Parmesan cheese

$1\frac{1}{2}$ teaspoons brown sugar

1 tablespoon minced garlic

$1\frac{1}{2}$ teaspoons cayenne

1 cup Madeira wine

8 chicken breasts

Oil for frying

Garnish: shaved goat cheese (optional)

1. Chop onions, and soak in milk for at least 1 hour.

2. Mix flour, cayenne, cumin, garlic powder, paprika, onion powder, and salt. Set aside.

3. In a large pot, reconstitute already de-seeded ancho chilies in 6 cups water. Remove chilies, and add demi-glace to water.

4. Mince chilies. Add them to the water–demi-glace mixture, along with goat cheese, Parmesan, brown sugar, garlic, cayenne, and wine. Bring to a slow boil, and reduce until slightly thickened.

5. Grill chicken breasts.

6. Coat soaked onions in flour mix, and deep fry.

7. Arrange breasts on a plate with saffron rice and black beans. Cover chicken with sauce, and top with onions. For an optional garnish, shave goat cheese on top.

**YIELD: 8 SERVINGS**

# ORANGE-CILANTRO ROASTED CHICKEN

## BARLEY & HOPPS BREWERY, SAN MATEO, CA

*This is an adaptation of an award-winning smoked duck recipe created by Executive Chef H. Thomas Halen. The chicken gains a wonderful flavor from the marinade, while retaining its moisture. The flavors are Southwestern, with a slight spiciness, making it a perfect complement with lighter ales and refreshing wheat beers.*

### MARINADE

6 cups water

2 cups orange juice

2 cups dry white wine

1 cup soy sauce

1 cup kosher salt

1 cup packed brown sugar

$\frac{1}{4}$ cup granulated onion

$\frac{1}{4}$ cup cracked peppercorns

$\frac{1}{4}$ cup granulated garlic

1 bunch cilantro, chopped

4 jalapeño peppers, seeded and chopped


6 half chickens

Freshly ground black pepper


1. Combine marinade ingredients. Add chickens, and marinate 4–6 hours or overnight.

2. Preheat oven to 375°F. Remove chickens from marinade, and discard marinade. Season with freshly ground black pepper.

3. Place chickens, skin side up, in roasting pan, and roast for 35–45 minutes or until done.

## PASILLA CHILI SAUCE

6 fresh pasilla chilies
Vegetable oil for coating chilies
2 tablespoons olive oil
$\frac{1}{2}$ cup diced yellow onion
3 garlic cloves
1 orange, zest and juice
2 cups chicken broth
$\frac{1}{8}$ teaspoon ground allspice
$\frac{1}{4}$ teaspoon ground cumin
$\frac{1}{8}$ teaspoon cayenne pepper
$\frac{1}{2}$ teaspoon black pepper
$1\frac{1}{2}$ teaspoons salt
2 tablespoons cilantro

1. Coat chilies with oil, and roast in broiler or on top of stove until skin is blistered and black. Place in a bowl, and cover with plastic wrap; let stand 15 minutes. Peel skin off peppers, and seed.

2. Meanwhile, heat olive oil in a saucepan. Add onions and garlic to hot oil. Sauté until onion is translucent. Add peeled pasilla chilies. Cook 2–3 minutes.

3. Add orange zest, orange juice, and chicken broth to saucepan. Bring to a boil, reduce heat, and simmer 5 minutes. Add remaining ingredients.

4. Place chili mixture into blender. Purée all ingredients until smooth.

5. Serve chicken with sauce.

YIELD: 6 SERVINGS

# GRILLED CHICKEN AND SWEET CORN RISOTTO

## TRIUMPH BREWING CO., PRINCETON, NJ

*Triumph prepares this entrée using chicken breasts with the wing bone attached for an attractive presentation, says Executive Chef Michael Perselay. You can assemble the dish as Triumph does—see the instructions in step 5 below—or you may substitute chicken cutlets or boneless chicken breast. Anchos are dried peppers that are slightly hot and sweet. The Ancho Broth can be prepared in advance. Make the ancho flakes for the risotto by crushing the dried ancho peppers. Chef Perselay recommends serving India pale ale or nut brown ale with this entrée.*

### ANCHO BROTH

4 dried ancho peppers

3 tomatoes

2 large carrots

2 medium onions

4 celery stalks

4 garlic cloves

2 quarts chicken stock

$\frac{1}{2}$ cup molasses

$\frac{1}{2}$ cup brown sugar

$\frac{1}{2}$ bunch cilantro, chopped

Salt and pepper to taste

### SWEET CORN RISOTTO

2 cups arborio rice

3 cups water

$\frac{1}{2}$ cup heavy cream

Kernels from 2 ears corn on the cob
1 teaspoon ancho pepper flakes (can substitute red pepper flakes)
$\frac{1}{2}$ bunch fresh tarragon, chopped
$\frac{1}{4}$ cup grated Parmesan cheese
Salt and pepper to taste

4 8-ounce chicken breasts, skin on, wing bone in
Garnish: chopped tarragon, ancho flakes

1. Prepare Ancho Broth: Chop peppers, tomatoes, carrots, onions, celery, and garlic. Place in a 6- to 8-quart stockpot. Add stock, molasses, and brown sugar. Bring to a boil, lower to a simmer, and reduce by half.

2. Stir in cilantro and salt and pepper. Blend in a food processor or blender until smooth. Strain through a strainer. (The sauce should be fairly thin in texture.) Reserve and keep warm.

3. Prepare Sweet Corn Risotto: Place the rice and water in a pot over low heat and cover, stirring occasionally. When the water is absorbed, add the heavy cream, corn, pepper flakes, and tarragon, stirring constantly. Add the cheese, folding in, and salt and pepper to taste.

4. Grill or broil chicken breasts.

5. To serve: Place the rice in the center of each of four plates or large, flat bowls. Cut the chicken breast on a bias from the bone to the tip, crosscut, making medallions. Place the chicken against the rice around the front, and ladle the sauce around the breast so that it spreads on the plate. Garnish with chopped tarragon and ancho flakes.

YIELD: 4 SERVINGS

# CHICKEN JALFRAJIE

## JAIPUR RESTAURANT AND BREWING CO., OMAHA, NE

*From the country's only brewpub that's also an Indian restaurant, Chef Raj Bhandari offers this spicy chicken dish. It's very quick and easy to prepare. Chef Bhandari recommends whole cumin seeds over ground for their fresher flavor. Serve it with rice and a light-bodied lager, to not overpower the intricate spices.*

1 pound boneless, skinless chicken breasts

2 tablespoons vegetable oil

Pinch whole cumin seeds

1½ teaspoons salt

¼ teaspoon turmeric

½ teaspoon red chili powder

3 tablespoons lemon juice

1 medium bell pepper

1 small onion

1 medium tomato

1. Cut the chicken breasts into bite-size pieces and wash them in cold water, then pat dry.

2. Heat the oil in a frying pan, and sauté the chicken with cumin seeds, salt, and turmeric for about 5 minutes. Add the chili powder and lemon juice, and let cook for about 2 minutes. Add water if needed.

3. Cut the bell pepper, onion, and tomato into bite-size pieces, and add them to the chicken. Cook until tender. Serve with rice.

**YIELD: 2 SERVINGS**

# CHAPTER 7
# MEAT ENTRÉES

The United States is the land of meat and potatoes. In the Midwest, you'll still find folks for whom the term "eating out" is synonymous with "eating steak." Fortunately, there are so many delicious ways to prepare pork and beef that even those who eat them only occasionally can enjoy them to the fullest.

While some of these dishes can be prepared fairly quickly, quite a few of them require some marination time. That's just the nature of the beast; if you try to hurry the entrées along, the meats won't soak up the full flavors of marinades.

Heartier beers, such as malty ales and lagers, will work well with nearly all of these dishes. Because the entrées are for the most part solid, stick-to-the-ribs dishes, consider serving smaller portions of beer with them.

# ITALIAN MEAT BALLS

*Pete's Place is a family-style Italian restaurant that has been around since 1925. Founder Pete Pritchard (formerly Pietro Piegari) homebrewed "choc beer" back in the 1910s and '20s, and began selling food to go along with it. These classic Italian meatballs can be served atop pasta or in a sandwich. Serve them with either a light ale or lager, or a malty amber lager or Märzen/Oktoberfest.*

1 pound ground meat

½ cup cracker crumbs

½ cup chopped onions

1 tablespoon grated Parmesan cheese

1 tablespoon chopped parsley

1 egg, beaten

2 teaspoons salt

1 teaspoon black pepper

½ clove garlic, puréed

Pasta sauce or peppers and onions

1. Preheat oven to 300°F. Mix all the ingredients by hand in a large bowl. Roll mixed meat into balls.

2. Bake until internal temperature is 160°F (use meat thermometer).

3. Serve with your favorite pasta sauce or with sautéed bell peppers and onions.

YIELD: 8–10 MEATBALLS

# BADLANDS PORK TENDERLOIN

RATTLESNAKE CREEK BREWERY
AND GRILL,
DICKINSON, ND

*This is the most popular item on the brewpub's current menu. It utilizes a teriyaki marinade, and though this recipe may sound complicated it is very easy to prepare. Pork tenderloin is absolutely the best cut of pork there is, and it is very tender and lean. Brewer Joel Anderson has this for dinner about once a week and says it is best eaten while sipping a red ale.*

1½ cups soy sauce

¾ cup canola oil

2 tablespoons honey

½ cup American brown ale

1 tablespoon minced garlic

½ teaspoon ground ginger

¼ teaspoon dried orange peel

2 pounds pork tenderloin

1. Combine all ingredients except pork in small saucepan, and bring to a boil. Allow to cool. Reserve ¼ cup marinade for serving over medallions.

2. Marinate tenderloins for 12–24 hours in a closed container in the refrigerator. To cook, broil tenderloins in a 495°F oven for 14 minutes. Slice into ½-inch medallions. Arrange on plate, and pour the reserved marinade on top.

**YIELD: 4 SERVINGS**

# PORK ROULADEN WITH DÜSSELDORF CREAM SAUCE

## THE BLACK ANGUS AT STOUDT BREWERY, ADAMSTOWN, PA

*After many trips to Germany, Ed and Carol Stoudt brought this favorite back to Adamstown. It is a big hit both in the Black Angus restaurant and Stoudt's Brew Pub. Bockwurst is a popular German pork-and-veal sausage. Stoudt's bottled beers are available in Pennsylvania and other Mid-Atlantic states. Serve this dish with a Märzen/Oktoberfest.*

1½ pounds boneless pork loin,
cut into 4 5-ounce portions and pounded flat
2 bunches spinach, washed and chopped
4 pieces bockwurst, 4 ounces each, casings removed
2 cups shredded Swiss cheese
Düsseldorf Cream (see recipe at right)

1. Preheat oven to 400°F. Lay pieces of pork tenderloin out flat. Divide spinach evenly among the tenderloins. Place a piece of bockwurst on the edge of each loin. Sprinkle top with Swiss cheese, and roll loin over itself to cover the entire mixture.

2. Bake for 15 minutes. Cut each Rouladen into ½-inch pieces. Lay each end-to-end in center of plate. Cover lightly with Düsseldorf Cream.

## DÜSSELDORF CREAM

1 quart heavy cream
2 cups Düsseldorf mustard

1. In a saucepan, heat cream over medium heat and reduce it by half, stirring. Add mustard until blended smoothly.

**YIELD: 4 SERVINGS**

# SHEPHERD'S PIE

## GRITTY MCDUFF'S BREW PUB, PORTLAND, ME

*This hearty main course is a favorite of customers at Gritty McDuff's. Several of Gritty McDuff's beers are bottled and distributed in the Northeast. Serve Shepherd's Pie with Gritty's Black Fly Stout or another stout.*

1½ pounds lean hamburger

⅓ cup diced onion

1 stalk celery, diced

2 teaspoons minced garlic

½ teaspoon thyme

1 teaspoon oregano

1½ teaspoons crushed red pepper

1 cup Gritty's Black Fly Stout or other stout

Salt and pepper to taste

3 pounds potatoes, peeled and cut into big chunks

¼ cup butter

⅓ cup milk

⅓ cup sour cream

2 tablespoons chives

1 16-ounce can whole kernel corn

2 16-ounce cans creamed corn

Paprika

YIELD: 8–10 SERVINGS

1. Sauté hamburger, onion, celery, garlic, thyme, oregano, red pepper, stout, and salt and pepper until meat is brown. Place sautéed burger mixture in large, shallow casserole dish.

2. Cook potatoes in water. Mash and season with butter, milk, sour cream, chives, and salt and pepper.

3. Preheat oven to 350°F. Drain corn, and mix with creamed corn. Layer corn mixture on burger mixture, and spread evenly. Layer on mashed potatoes. Sprinkle paprika lightly over top.

4. Bake for about 20 minutes.

# BAVARIAN POT ROAST WITH STOUT GRAVY

## LEAVENWORTH BREWERY, LEAVENWORTH, WA

*This succulent pot roast is basted with stout and served with carrots, potatoes, and stout gravy. It goes well with a dunkelweizen, porter, or stout.*

Pot roast, 5–7 pounds

Seasoning salt

Italian seasoning

Black pepper

Onion powder

Garlic powder

1 pint stout

$6\frac{1}{2}$ cups water, plus water to cover vegetables

10–12 carrots, sliced

10–12 small potatoes, sliced

$\frac{1}{4}$ cup flour

Beef bouillon cube (optional)

Salt and pepper

**YIELD: 10–14 SERVINGS**

1. Preheat oven to 350°F. Coat the entire roast with the seasoning salt of your choice, Italian seasoning, black pepper, onion powder, and garlic powder. Place the seasoned roast in a large roasting pan.

2. Add stout and 6 cups water. Cover and bake for 3–4 hours. Check during baking time, and add more water if level drops below half of roast.

3. During the last 1–$1\frac{1}{2}$ hours of baking, add sliced carrots and potatoes, and add water to cover the vegetables. Continue cooking until the vegetables are tender.

4. Make gravy: Pour cooking liquid into a saucepan, and bring to a boil. In a small bowl, thoroughly mix flour and $\frac{1}{2}$ cup water. Add gradually to the boiling stock. Stir until thick. You may add 1 bouillon cube and salt and pepper to taste.

# BEEF WITH BLACK RADISH BEER

## WEEPING RADISH BREWERY, MANTEO, NC

*Weeping Radish owner Uli Bennewitz says this was one of his and his siblings' favorite meals as children living and growing up in the mountains of Bavaria. This dish can be served with spaetzle, rice, pasta, mashed potatoes, or French bread. Weeping Radish's Black Radish Beer is bottled and sold on the East Coast. Serve the beef with a dunkelweizen at lunch, or a dark lager, stout, or doppelbock at dinner.*

$\frac{1}{2}$ pound bacon, cut into 1-inch pieces

30 small white onions

3 pounds beef rump, cut into 3-inch chunks

1 cup plus 2 tablespoons flour

1 large onion, chopped

3 cups Weeping Radish Black Radish Beer, or other dark lager

2 garlic cloves, crushed

1 teaspoon salt

$\frac{1}{2}$ teaspoon thyme

1 teaspoon pepper

1 bay leaf

1 pound mushrooms, sliced

4 tablespoons butter or margarine

1. In large Dutch oven, cook bacon pieces over medium heat until browned. Remove bacon onto paper towel to drain. Set aside. Leave about $\frac{1}{4}$ cup of drippings in Dutch oven in which to cook white onions.

2. Add white onions to Dutch oven and sauté until lightly browned. Place onions in a small bowl; set aside.

3. In large bowl or on waxed paper, coat meat chunks with 1 cup flour. Using drippings in Dutch oven over medium-high heat, cook meat, several pieces at a time, until browned on all sides. Remove pieces as they brown.

4. Sauté chopped onion in Dutch oven over medium heat for about 5 minutes. Preheat the oven to 325°F. Return the beef to the Dutch oven, pour in the beer, and add reserved bacon, garlic, salt, thyme, pepper, and bay leaf. Place Dutch oven in oven, and bake for 3–3½ hours.

5. About 1 hour before meat is cooked, sauté mushrooms in 2 tablespoons melted butter or margarine until golden brown, about 6–8 minutes. Place in a small bowl.

6. In another small bowl, combine 2 tablespoons softened butter or margarine and 2 tablespoons flour, and mix until smooth.

7. Take Dutch oven out of oven. Add flour-butter mixture, ½ teaspoon at a time, to the mixture in the oven, stirring until blended after each addition. Add onions and mushrooms to Dutch oven. Return to oven and cook for 1 more hour.

YIELD: 8 SERVINGS

# SPIESSBRATEN

## SUDWERK PRIVATBRAUEREI HÜBSCH, DAVIS, CA

*This traditional German dish, developed by Chef Gretel Henrichs, can be served with hot German potato salad and red cabbage, or you can Americanize it by serving it with home fries or mashed potatoes. You cannot have too many onions in this dish. MAGGI is a liquid seasoning available at many supermarkets and specialty food stores. It also makes a good base for gravy and all-around seasoning. Note the longer-than-usual marination time for this recipe. Serve Spiessbraten with any German-style beer, such as a pilsner, Continental or dark lager, or Märzen/Oktoberfest.*

3 cups thinly sliced yellow onions

$\frac{1}{4}$ cup chopped garlic

$1\frac{1}{2}$ teaspoons salt

2 teaspoons sugar

1 teaspoon black pepper

$\frac{1}{4}$ cup MAGGI liquid seasoning

$\frac{1}{2}$ cup oil

4 pork steaks, cut about $\frac{1}{2}$-inch thick
(approximately 10 ounces each)

2 tablespoons butter

1. In a large bowl, mix all ingredients except pork and butter.

2. In a separate container, smother the pork steaks in the onion mixture. Seal and refrigerate for 48–72 hours.

3. Preheat oven to 350°F or prepare barbecue grill. Remove the pork steaks from onion mixture, making sure there are no onions on the steaks.

PRIVATBRAUEREI

Sudwerk

HÜBSCH

4. Using a colander, drain all the liquid off the onions.

5. Grill pork steaks for 12–15 minutes. While the steaks are cooking, sauté the onions in butter until they start to brown.

6. Serve pork steaks with the sautéed onions on top.

YIELD: 4 SERVINGS

# BUFFALO OR BEEF BRISKET

## FIREHOUSE BREWING CO., RAPID CITY, SD

*Chef Lawrence Duckett says this recipe came about when a meat-cutting company asked him if he could use some buffalo brisket. He did some test recipes and came up with this dish. The flavor of the sauce is a cross between Hawaiian and Korean, which complements the buffalo to the fullest. If you cannot get buffalo, use beef brisket. The brewpub serves Firehouse Chukkar Ale, a wheat beer, with this dish.*

5 pounds brisket

2 cups wheat beer

$\frac{1}{4}$ cup lemon juice

1 cup soy sauce

1 cup brown sugar

1 tablespoon freshly minced garlic

$1\frac{1}{2}$ teaspoons freshly grated ginger

$1\frac{1}{2}$ teaspoons salt

$1\frac{1}{2}$ teaspoons black pepper

2 green onions, chopped

2 tablespoons cornstarch

YIELD: 8–10 SERVINGS

1. Wash brisket and trim off excess fat. Place in oven-proof baking dish.

2. Mix remaining ingredients, except for cornstarch, in a bowl. Adjust seasonings as needed. Pour marinade over brisket, and marinate, covered, overnight in refrigerator.

3. Preheat oven to 350°F. Bake until tender, about 2 hours. Let meat sit in marinade while it cools down. Slice and place on serving platter.

4. Place marinade in a saucepan, and heat it to boiling. Mix cornstarch with some cold water. Add cornstarch mixture slowly to boiling liquid until it becomes thick enough to coat the back of a spoon. Pour some sauce over the brisket, and serve the remainder with the meal.

# BABY BACK RIBS WITH STODDARD'S BREW BBQ SAUCE

## STODDARD'S BREWHOUSE AND EATERY, SUNNYVALE, CA

*At Stoddard's Brewhouse, these barbecued ribs have become very popular. At the brewhouse they are served with home-made fries, coleslaw, and a side of barbecue sauce. Chipotle peppers are available in specialty food stores and in the Mexican section of many supermarkets. Try a malty amber ale or lager, a roasty porter, or even a smoked beer with these ribs.*

### SAUCE

36 ounces ketchup

3 tablespoons tomato paste

3 tablespoons smoked chipotle peppers

$\frac{1}{2}$ cup white wine vinegar

$\frac{1}{3}$ cup cider vinegar

3 tablespoons dry mustard

$\frac{1}{4}$ cup kosher salt

3 tablespoon chili powder

2 tablespoons black pepper

1 tablespoon plus 1 teaspoon Tabasco sauce

1 cup dark beer

$\frac{1}{3}$ cup Worcestershire sauce

$\frac{1}{4}$ cup peanut oil

5 tablespoons barbecue spice

3 tablespoons molasses

3 tablespoons brown sugar

1. Place all ingredients in a large bowl and blend. Let sit for at least 4 hours. The longer you let the sauce sit, the better it will be.

## RIBS

2 large slabs of baby back ribs, 1¾ pounds or more

1. Place ribs in a small, shallow container. Pour on the barbecue sauce, cover, and marinate for 1 day in the refrigerator.

2. When ready to cook, preheat oven to 320°F and place ribs on a sheet pan. Bake for 1½ hours.

## COLESLAW

3 cups sour cream

3 cups mayonnaise

2 teaspoons salt

3 tablespoons dry mustard

¼ cup sugar

3 tablespoons horseradish

1 teaspoon black pepper

1 small yellow onion

1 tablespoon chopped fresh parsley

⅓ cup cider vinegar

¼ cup apple juice

⅓ cup pineapple juice

2 large heads of green cabbage, shredded

1. In a large bowl, mix sour cream, mayonnaise, salt, dry mustard, sugar, horseradish, and black pepper.

2. Grind the onion in a food processor. Add in the parsley, cider vinegar, apple juice, and pineapple juice. Let sit for about 20 minutes.

3. Place the shredded cabbage in a large bowl. Add the dressing to your taste.

YIELD: 2 SLABS RIBS, SERVING 2–4

# STEAK WITH ALOHA ALE SAUCE

## GENTLEMAN JIM'S BISTRO AND BREWERY, POUGHKEEPSIE, NY

*This steak sauce can be used with any cut of steak you wish. Gentleman Jim's uses it with sliced butt steak. The recipe will make enough for 5–6 pounds of meat, and you can refrigerate any sauce that's left over. Serve this dish with a brown ale, porter, or stout.*

1½ cups pineapple juice

¼ cup soy sauce

3½ tablespoons light brown sugar

¼ teaspoon powdered garlic

¼ teaspoon ground ginger

¼ cup porter or other dark beer

2 teaspoons cornstarch

Steak

1. Mix together juice, soy sauce, brown sugar, garlic, and ginger. Bring to a boil.

2. In a small bowl, stir together beer and cornstarch. Add to mixture. Lower heat, and cook, stirring, until sauce is thickened. Don't let the mixture boil after adding the beer.

3. Cook steak to desired doneness. Serve sauce under, over, or in a small container beside the steak.

**YIELD: ABOUT 2 CUPS, ENOUGH FOR 5–6 POUNDS OF MEAT OR 10–12 SERVINGS**

# CHAPTER 8
## DESSERTS

airing sweet beers with sweet foods is a satisfying way to end an elegant meal, and the pairings are easy. Think fruit-flavored beers with fruity desserts, malty bocks with caramel or nut-based desserts, and malty brown ales or any kind of stout with chocolate desserts. In most cases (an exception being Goose Island's Cascade Pumpkin Brûlée, p. 134), stay away from beers with substantial hop flavor.

For a lighter end to the meal, consider serving beer as dessert. Choose a strong beer, such as a barley wine, Russian imperial stout, or strong ale, and serve it in a small glass. The alcohol content will warm your guests down to their toes. In warmer weather, try a fruit-flavored lambic. Nothing says "the meal is over" quite like a superb lambic, because anything that follows it will pale in comparison.

# CHOCOLATE TRUFFLES

## TABLEROCK BREWPUB & GRILL, BOISE, ID

*Yes, beer and chocolate! TableRock serves these candies around Valentine's Day with glasses of Shillelagh Stout. A stout, porter, or fruity lambic will accompany these nicely.*

1 pound bittersweet chocolate
$\frac{1}{2}$ cup heavy cream
$\frac{1}{4}$ cup powdered sugar
2 tablespoons stout
$\frac{1}{4}$ cup butter, softened
Cocoa powder

1. Melt chocolate in double boiler.

2. Gently heat the cream in a saucepan.

3. After the chocolate is melted, mix in the powdered sugar, warmed cream, stout, and butter. Stir until just mixed. Do not overmix. Refrigerate until the mixture is cold and firm.

4. Scoop out chocolate mixture by the tablespoonful, and roll into bite-sized balls. Roll the balls in cocoa powder to coat. Place on wax paper. Serve, or store in the refrigerator.

**YIELD: APPROXIMATELY 5 DOZEN BITE-SIZED TRUFFLES**

# THE DOUBLE TRIPLE

## GREAT NORTHERN RESTAURANT & BREWERY, FARGO, ND

*This dessert gets its name from the use of two bottles of Mackeson's XXX Stout, a cream stout made in England. You may substitute another cream stout. The unusual flavor of the stout nicely complements the sweet cream mixture and ladyfingers. Serve this with a sweet stout, Russian imperial stout, porter, raspberry ale, or malty lager such as a bock.*

2 pounds mascarpone cheese or cream cheese, softened

2 eggs

1 cup powdered sugar

2 12-ounce bottles Mackeson XXX Stout

$1\frac{1}{2}$ cups sugar

2 teaspoons vanilla

2 dozen ladyfingers

1. Whip cheese, eggs, and powdered sugar in a mixer just until fluffy. Set aside.

2. Cook beer and sugar in a saucepan over medium heat until syrupy. Remove from heat, and add vanilla. Cool syrup in refrigerator.

3. To prepare: Dip half of the ladyfingers in the stout syrup, and place in a 13x9 pan. Put half of the filling on top. Repeat with remaining ladyfingers and filling.

4. Chill in refrigerator for 2 hours or until set.

**YIELD: 12 SERVINGS**

# CHOCOLATE CALZONE

## VINO'S BREWPUB, LITTLE ROCK, AR

*This is definitely not for the low-cal crowd, but the chocolate-loving sweets-eaters will certainly dig in! You can use a pre-made pizza dough (enough for a 16-inch crust) or pastry dough, or make the pizza dough at right. A nice hazelnut brown ale complements the chocolate perfectly. Vino's owner Henry Lee says, "Thanks to the folks at River Market Brewing Co. in Kansas City, Mo., for the inspiration for this one."*

1 ball Pizza Dough (see recipe at right), or your favorite pizza or pastry dough

$\frac{1}{4}$ cup sugar

$\frac{3}{4}$ cup semisweet chocolate chips

$\frac{1}{2}$ teaspoon vanilla extract

Pinch cinnamon

2 teaspoons shredded coconut

1 cup ricotta cheese

Garnish: chocolate syrup, chopped pecans, powdered sugar

1. Preheat oven to 450°F. Place dough on a lightly floured surface. Press down and form into a circle. Using a floured rolling pin, roll dough into a 16-inch circle, $\frac{1}{8}$-inch to $\frac{1}{4}$-inch thick. Sprinkle with a pinch of sugar and press it into dough. Cut circle in half.

2. Combine sugar, chocolate chips, vanilla, cinnamon, coconut, and ricotta cheese. Place half of mixture on each dough piece. Fold dough crosswise over filling. Cut edges of dough so that they are even. (Each piece should look like a crescent.)

3. Seal edges well with the tines of a fork. Fold approximately $\frac{3}{8}$ inch of the edge back over itself. Seal again with the fork, to be sure it's sealed well (or you'll have a real mess).

4. Place on lightly greased baking sheet, and bake until golden brown, approximately 8–10 minutes.

5. Place on plate, and drizzle chocolate syrup in zigzag pattern over calzone. Top with chopped pecans and powdered sugar.

## PIZZA DOUGH

1 cup warm water (110°F –115°F)
$\frac{1}{4}$-ounce package dry yeast
$3\frac{1}{4}$ cups flour (approximately), plus
$\frac{1}{4}$ cup for work surface
1 teaspoon salt
$\frac{1}{4}$ cup olive oil (less 2 tablespoons
measured separately)

1. Place water in small bowl. Add yeast and stir until a beige mixture forms. Let stand until a light layer of foam forms, approximately 5 minutes.

2. Combine 3 cups flour with salt in large mixing bowl. Make a well in the center, and add yeast mixture and oil. Stir flour into the liquid until it is mixed well and a soft dough forms. Turn the dough onto a floured work surface and knead, slowly adding remaining $\frac{1}{4}$ cup flour until the dough is no longer sticky. Knead just until the dough is smooth and elastic and all visible flour is incorporated. Shape the dough into a ball, and place into another bowl oiled with the remaining 2 tablespoons oil. Roll ball around to coat evenly.

3. Cover bowl with plastic wrap, place in a warm, draft-free location, and let rise until doubled in size. Punch down and knead another minute before using.

**YIELD: 4 SERVINGS**

# LEMON-ORANGE PUDDING CAKE

## GORDON BIERSCH, HONOLULU, HI

*This dessert features a light sponge cake texture, scented with the citrus flavors of lemon and orange, with a delectable pudding surprise. The batter separates while baking, to create a light cake on the top and a creamy pudding on the bottom. Pair the cakes with a Belgian wit or a fruit beer.*

$\frac{1}{2}$ cup butter

1$\frac{1}{2}$ cups sugar

6 eggs, separated

$\frac{1}{3}$ cup lemon juice

$\frac{1}{3}$ cup orange juice

2 tablespoons finely minced orange zest

$\frac{1}{2}$ teaspoon salt

3 cups milk

$\frac{2}{3}$ cup flour, sifted

Powdered sugar

1. Preheat oven to 350° F. Cream butter and sugar until light and fluffy. Scrape down bowl, and add egg yolks, one at a time. Scrape down bowl again, and add juices, orange zest, and salt. Add milk.

2. With clean beaters, mix egg whites on low until foamy, then whip on high until soft peaks form.

3. Fold flour and egg whites into egg yolk mixture, alternating between flour and whites. Be gentle about mixing in the egg whites—they will deflate if overmixed.

4. Divide mixture among individual soufflé dishes (6–8-ounce ovenproof dishes). Place dishes in a large roasting pan. Create a water bath by pouring hot water in the pan so that it is halfway up the sides of the dishes.

5. Bake for 35–40 minutes, or until the cakes are puffed and golden. Serve warm, dusted with powdered sugar.

YIELD: 8–10 SERVINGS

# CHOCOLATE STOUT TORTE

## DEMPSEYS ALEHOUSE AT SONOMA BREWING CO., PETALUMA, CA

*This light, flavorful cake is quite popular at Dempsey's. The brewpub serves it in a pool of chocolate sauce and with a scoop of homemade stout ice cream (see Phoenix Brewing's on page 137). Serve a glass of stout alongside.*

6 ounces semisweet chocolate

3 ounces butter

$\frac{1}{4}$ cup stout

1 cup sugar

4 egg yolks

4 egg whites

2 cups toasted pecans, ground fine

Pinch of salt

1. Preheat oven to 350°F. Lightly butter a 9-inch springform pan.

2. In the top of a double boiler, melt together the chocolate, butter, and stout.

**YIELD: 1 9-INCH CAKE**

3. While these are melting, whip egg yolks and $\frac{1}{2}$ cup sugar with an electric mixer until mixture is pale yellow and has doubled in volume. Set aside.

4. With clean beaters, whip whites with the other $\frac{1}{2}$ cup sugar until soft peaks form.

5. Remove chocolate mixture from heat; cool slightly. Mix the chocolate mixture and pecans into yolks, and stir to incorporate.

6. Gently fold in egg whites, a third at a time, until all are incorporated. Add salt.

7. Pour batter into prepared pan, and bake for 45 minutes, or until toothpick inserted in center comes out almost clean. This cake will rise and fall as it cooks, and that is okay.

# STOUT CHEESECAKE

## COMMONWEALTH BREWING CO., BOSTON, MA

*Stout and chocolate come together in this rich cheesecake with an Oreo crust, developed by Commonwealth's Executive Chef, Glenn Jordan. Serve it with a stout.*

### CRUST

1½ cups Oreo cookie crumbs

2 tablespoons melted butter

### FILLING

3 pounds cream cheese

1⅞ cups sugar

Pinch salt

1½ teaspoons cornstarch

Juice of 2 lemons

4 eggs

½ cup heavy cream

1 cup stout

Garnish: fruit

1. Combine crust ingredients, and press firmly into the bottom of a 9-inch springform pan, making sure to seal edges with crumbs.

2. Soften cream cheese in mixer until smooth with no lumps. Add sugar, and mix until smooth. Add salt, cornstarch, and lemon juice, and mix at medium-low speed.

3. Add eggs, one at a time, scraping sides of mixing bowl occasionally and fully incorporating each egg before adding the next.

4. Add heavy cream, and mix thoroughly. Add stout, and mix thoroughly. Pour into crust.

5. Bake at 425°F in conventional oven, or 400°F in convection oven, for 8 minutes, or until golden brown on top. Lower temperature to 225°F (200°F convection), and bake 1 hour and 15 minutes. Let cool for 3 hours before serving. Garnish with fruit of choice.

YIELD: 1 9-INCH CHEESECAKE

# CASCADE PUMPKIN BRÛLÉE

## GOOSE ISLAND BREWING CO., CHICAGO, IL

*Purchase Cascade hops at your local homebrew store. Bury the eggs in a container with the Cascade hops, seal, and refrigerate for 3–5 days. Goose Island Brewmaster Greg Hall says that because eggs are porous, they will breathe the hops aroma, which is similar to pine, and the aroma will perfume the eggs. He recommends serving Goose Island's Christmas Ale, which is available in bottles during the holiday season, or an extra special bitter with the brûlée.*

10 eggs

$\frac{1}{2}$ pound Cascade hops (either pellets or whole hops)

$\frac{1}{2}$ pound cooked pumpkin or butternut squash, puréed

$\frac{1}{2}$ cup milk

2 cups heavy cream

$\frac{1}{2}$ cup sugar

2 vanilla beans, split lengthwise

Pinch of salt

Pinch of nutmeg

Pinch of cinnamon

$\frac{1}{4}$ pound brown sugar

1. Seal the eggs in a container with the Cascade hops for 3–5 days (see note above).

2. Place all ingredients except eggs and brown sugar in a heavy-bottomed medium saucepan. Bring to a boil over medium heat.

3. Remove from heat, and let sit so the beans can steep for at least 1 hour, or until mixture cools to room temperature.

4. Strain mixture through a mesh sieve, discard the vanilla beans, and gently push the pumpkin through the sieve.

5. Preheat oven to 300°F. Pour $\frac{1}{2}$ inch hot water into a 2-inch deep, 13x21 baking dish (or use two smaller baking dishes). Place in oven for 15 minutes.

6. Separate Cascade-scented eggs, discarding the whites. Whisk the egg yolks into the cooked mixture, and strain again through a fine mesh sieve.

7. Pour mixture into 8 4-ounce brûlée dishes or soufflé cups. Place dishes in the water-filled baking dish in the oven. Bake until the custard sets, about 45–60 minutes. When it has set, a knife inserted into the center will come out dry. Remove brûlée dishes from the water bath, and cool at room temperature for 15 minutes. Cover and refrigerate for at least 1 hour before serving. (Steps 2–7 can be done a day in advance.)

8. To serve: Sprinkle the brown sugar evenly across the tops of the brûlées. Be careful not to clump the sugar. A propane torch works best for the "brûléeing," but your oven broiler may be used as well. Place under the flame or heating coil for about 30 seconds, or until sugar is evenly caramelized. Serve immediately.

YIELD: 8 SERVINGS

# BLACK STOUT PECAN PIE WITH OATMEAL STOUT ICE CREAM

## PHOENIX BREWING CO., ATLANTA, GA

*Executive chef Kevin Fonzo and pastry chef Karsten Krivenko combined their talents to come up with this dessert. They describe it as "probably the biggest-selling dessert at the Phoenix, and the most unique." The beer gives the ice cream a malty, almost coffee-like taste. Of course, you can make the pie without the ice cream, but for the ultimate decadence, make the ice cream, too. Serve it with an oatmeal stout, and you have the ultimate "death by stout."*

### BLACK STOUT PECAN PIE

5 eggs

1⅓ cups dark corn syrup

1⅓ cups sugar

1 teaspoon vanilla

3 tablespoons butter, melted

½ cup stout

3 cups pecans

1 10-inch pie crust, unbaked

1. Preheat oven to 350°F. Beat eggs lightly. Add corn syrup, sugar, vanilla, butter, and stout. Mix until well blended. Fold in pecans.

2. Turn mixture into pie crust, and bake for 45–55 minutes, or until set. Let cool before cutting.

**YIELD: 1 10-INCH PIE**

# OATMEAL STOUT ICE CREAM

1 quart milk
1 quart heavy cream
1 cup oatmeal stout
$\frac{1}{2}$ cup dark corn syrup
8 egg yolks
2 vanilla beans, seeds scraped out
1 cup sugar

1. In medium saucepan, heat milk and heavy cream.

2. In separate saucepan, bring stout to a boil and reduce to $\frac{1}{2}$ cup. Stir in corn syrup. Remove from heat.

3. Combine egg yolks, vanilla bean seeds, and sugar in a heat-proof bowl.

4. When cream mixture comes to a boil, add hot cream mixture to egg yolk-sugar-vanilla mixture, 1 cup at a time, mixing well between additions. When the cream mixture is incorporated, strain. Cool completely.

5. Gently whip stout mixture into cream mixture. Freeze mixture in ice cream freezer, following manufacturer's directions.

YIELD: 1 HALF-GALLON

# TOFFEE PUDDING

## ST. LOUIS BREWERY AND TAP ROOM, ST. LOUIS, MO

*Called "Sticky Toffee Pudding" at the brewpub, this dish is not a pudding in the American sense of the word, but a dense, rich date cake warmed by a hot caramel sauce and accompanied by a cool scoop of homemade whipped cream. The Tap Room's kitchen is probably best known for this dessert of Scottish origins, and has won more than a few awards for it as well. A hearty stout or English-style pale ale goes best with this rich, warm dessert.*

1½ pounds dried dates, chopped

4 cups hot water

4 teaspoons baking soda

1½ pounds superfine sugar

½ pound unsalted butter, plus extra to coat pan

8 large eggs

½ pound flour, plus extra to coat pan

2 teaspoons baking powder

½ teaspoon salt

2 teaspoons vanilla extract

Caramel Sauce (see recipe at right)

Homemade Whipped Cream (see recipe on page 140)

1. Preheat oven to 350°F. Grease pan (large enough to hold about 4 pounds of batter) with butter, and coat with flour, shaking out excess.

2. Combine dates and hot water in a saucepan, and bring to a boil. Stir with wire whisk to dissolve dates until smooth. Remove from heat, and add baking soda. Set aside to cool.

3. With an electric mixer on high speed, cream the sugar and butter 3 minutes.

4. With mixer on low speed, add eggs, one by one, and blend. When well combined, add flour, baking powder, and salt. Add the cooled dates with liquid, and vanilla.

5. Transfer mixture to baking pan and place in preheated oven. Bake until firm and toothpick inserted in center comes out clean, 35–50 minutes. When cool, cut into 12 squares.

6. To serve: Place one portion of cake on each plate. Using a 4-ounce ladle, pour hot Caramel Sauce over cake. Place dollop of Homemade Whipped Cream alongside the cake.

## CARAMEL SAUCE

$1\frac{1}{4}$ pounds brown sugar
$\frac{3}{4}$ pound butter
$1\frac{1}{2}$ teaspoons vanilla extract
1 cup heavy cream

1. In saucepan, stir together sugar, butter, and vanilla over low heat, stirring until butter is melted and brown sugar has completely dissolved.

2. Whisk in cream and blend thoroughly. Remove from heat.

3. The caramel sauce is poured over each piece individually at serving time and should be hot. It must be stirred frequently while being kept warm, which can be done in a double boiler. Individual servings may be microwaved.

# HOMEMADE WHIPPED CREAM

1 quart heavy cream
1 cup powdered sugar
1 tablespoon pure vanilla extract

1. Chill mixer blades and bowl in refrigerator.

2. Whip cream on high speed until it holds stiff peaks.

3. Fold in sugar and vanilla on low speed.

**YIELD: 12 SERVINGS**

# APPENDIX

## BEER STYLES DEFINED, AND COMMERCIAL EXAMPLES OF BEER STYLES

While brewpubs use their own beers to cook and pair with food, off-premise consumers can find beers of similar styles in their local package stores. Below are some of the more common beer styles and commercial examples of each. The beers listed were selected because they are distributed regionally or nationally.

Many of the brewpubs featured in this cookbook are also bottling microbreweries. You may find their products on your local store shelves. If not, feel free to substitute in the recipes other beers distributed in your state or region.

Parenthetical notations indicate the state or country in which the beer is brewed. Contract brewers and major brewing corporations are listed by the state or country where the corporation's headquarters are located.

## ALES

Full of fruitiness and flavor, ales can range in color from very light yellow to amber or dark brown.

**BLONDE OR GOLDEN ALE.** Light-colored beer with light-to-medium maltiness and/or hoppiness, light body, some fruitiness. Those in the microbrewing industry call it a "training wheel" beer, because its mild taste appeals to novice beer drinkers. Popular brewpub style. Brands: Genesee 12-Horse Ale (NY), Catamount Gold (VT), Full Sail Golden Ale (OR), Sea Dog Windjammer Blonde Ale (ME).

**AMBER ALE.** Medium-bodied beer, medium to high maltiness, hoppy in flavor and aroma. Can range in color from deep gold to light brown. Also popular at brewpubs. Brands: New Amsterdam Amber (NY), New Belgium Fat Tire Amber Ale (CO), Portland MacTarnahan's Amber Ale (OR), Boulder Amber Ale (CO).

**BITTER.** An English-style, gold- to copper-colored ale, with a pronounced hoppiness and often hints of caramel. Bitters are described as "ordinary," "special," or "extra special," depending on their maltiness, hoppiness, or strength. Fruity and hoppy aroma. Brands: Shipyard Old Thumper Extra Special Ale (ME), Fuller's London Pride (England), Redhook ESB (WA and NH), Left Hand Sawtooth Ale (CO), Boulder ESB (CO).

**PALE ALE.** Can range from golden to deep amber in color. Pronounced hoppy bitterness, low to medium malt, fruity or citruslike aroma. Brands: Summit Extra Pale Ale (MN), Sierra Nevada Pale Ale (CA), McAuslan St. Ambroise Pale Ale (Canada), Bass (England), Pete's Wicked Pale Ale (CA).

**INDIA PALE ALE.** Highly hopped pale ale, medium-bodied, higher in alcohol than classic pale ale. Golden to deep copper color. Flowery hoppiness, fruity or citrusy nose. Brands: Brooklyn East India Pale Ale (NY), Geary's India Pale Ale (ME), Grant's India Pale Ale (WA), Rogue I$^2$PA (OR), Anchor Liberty Ale (CA).

**ENGLISH BROWN ALE.** Medium-bodied and malty, very light on the hops. Mild aroma. Can range in color from copper to deep brown, with low to medium alcohol content. Brands: Newcastle Brown Ale (England), Samuel Smith's Nut Brown Ale (England), Lost Coast Downtown Brown (CA), Goose Island Hex Nut Brown Ale (IL).

**AMERICAN BROWN ALE.** Similar to its English cousin but with more hop aroma and bitterness. Brands: Pete's Wicked Ale (CA), Brooklyn Brown Ale (NY), Pyramid Best Brown (WA).

**OLD ALE.** Amber to dark brown in color, medium- to full-bodied, very malty aroma with hints of ripe fruit, alcohol taste. Brands: Theakston Old Peculier (England), Thomas Hardy's Ale (England), Bell's Third Coast Old Ale (MI).

**BARLEY WINE.** Very strong beer with lots of malt and hops. Copper to deep amber in color, warming, significant alcohol taste. Aroma can be strong on hops, malty, raisiny. Brands: Sierra Nevada Big Foot Barleywine Style Ale (CA),

Rogue Old Crustacean Barleywine (OR), Anchor Old Foghorn Barleywine Style Ale (CA), Young's Old Nick Barley Wine Style Ale (England).

## STOUT

Dark brown to black-colored ale. Body can range from medium to full. Very malty and hoppy.

**DRY STOUT.** Roasted barley gives dry stout its distinctive flavor. Made with plenty of hops, but hop bitterness is offset by the extreme maltiness. Aroma calls to mind coffee or burnt toast. Brands: Guinness Stout (Ireland), Shipyard Blue Fin Stout (ME), Sierra Nevada Stout (CA), North Coast Old No. 38 Stout (CA).

**SWEET OR MILK STOUT.** Lactose gives these stouts their creamy character. Tastes mildly of roasted barley, but very sweet. Nose of bitter chocolate or licorice. Brands: Whitbread Mackeson Stout (England), Samuel Adams Cream Stout (MA), Old Dominion Stout (VA), Elm City Blackwell Stout (CT).

**IMPERIAL STOUT.** Strong, sweet, "chewy" stout, originally brewed for Russian royalty. Complex flavor and aroma may include hints of chocolate, coffee, or licorice; high in alcohol. Brands: Rogue Imperial Stout (OR), Samuel Smith's Imperial Stout (England), Brooklyn Black Chocolate Stout (NY), North Coast Old Rasputin Russian Imperial Stout (CA), Grant's Imperial Stout (WA).

**OATMEAL STOUT.** Any stout that has been brewed with oats in addition to barley. Brands: Anderson Valley Barney Flats Oatmeal Stout (CA), McAuslan's St. Ambroise Oatmeal Stout (Canada), Young's Oatmeal Stout (England), Oasis Zoser Stout (CO).

## PORTER

Medium brown to nearly black beer, often lighter in body and drier than a stout. Aroma of roasted malt, hops, mild fruitiness.

**BROWN PORTER.** Medium to dark brown, with a sweet, often coffeelike taste and medium hoppiness. Brands: Anchor Porter (CA), Chicago Brewing Big Shoulders Porter (IL), Great Lakes Brewing Edmund Fitzgerald Porter (OH), Redhook Blackhook Porter (WA and NH).

**ROBUST PORTER.** Nearly black, with a bitter, burnt-malt taste. Medium to high hop bitterness. Brands: Left Hand Black Jack Porter (CO), Anderson Valley Deep Enders Dark Porter (CA).

## WHEAT BEERS

Popular brewpub beers made with a significant percentage of malted wheat, usually low in alcohol.

**WEISSBIER (ALSO CALLED WEIZENBIER).** Brewed with yeast that imparts the aroma of banana and cloves to the beer. Light-colored and light- to medium-bodied, fruity, with light maltiness, little hops. If the yeast is not filtered out, it is called hefeweiss or hefeweizen, and the banana-clove notes come through in the flavor as well. Brands: Erdinger Weiss (Germany), Tabernash Weiss (CO), Paulaner Hefe-Weizen (Germany).

**AMERICAN WHEAT ALE OR LAGER.** Higher amounts of hops and carbonation than the German-style wheat beers, often filtered. Color can range from straw to light amber. Light to medium body. Brewed with regular ale yeast, so it lacks the yeast flavor and aroma of the German-style wheats. Brands: Spanish Peaks Sweetwater Wheat Ale (MT), Widmer Hefeweizen (OR), Pyramid Wheaten Ale (WA), Catamount Summer Wheat (VT), Redhook Wheathook Ale (WA and NH).

**DUNKELWEISS (OR DUNKELWEIZEN).** A wheat beer made with a bit of roasted malt. Deep copper to brown, with a yeast-induced scent of cloves and maltiness in the nose and a malty flavor. Brands: Erdinger Dunkel (Germany), Schneider Dunkel Weisse (Germany), Sprecher Dunkel Weizen (WI).

## BELGIAN-STYLE ALES

Belgian ales share a distinctive aroma that derives from special yeast strains. Among the many beers in this category are:

BELGIAN WIT. Hazy, very pale beer with a spicy nose, light to medium body, dry finish. Often spiced with coriander and orange peel. Brands: Celis White (TX), New Belgium Sunshine Wheat (CO), Coors Blue Moon Belgian White (CO), Spring Street Wit (NY), Thomas Kemper Belgian White (WA).

LAMBIC. Cloudy, intensely sour beer made with wild yeasts and at least 30 percent raw wheat. Unblended lambics are rare in the United States. Gueuze is a mixture of young and old lambic. Faro is lambic with Belgian candi sugar added: Brands: Cantillon Lambic (Belgium), Boon Gueuze (Belgium), Boon Faro Pertotale (Belgium).

## LAGERS

Lagers are bottom-fermenting beers that ferment and are aged at cooler temperatures than ales.

AMERICAN LAGER. Light- to golden-colored, mildly malt- and hop-flavored, highly carbonated beer, usually brewed with adjuncts such as corn and rice. Brands: Budweiser (MO), Miller Genuine Draft (WI), Original Coors (CO).

AMERICAN LIGHT LAGER. What is known as "light beer," which is usually a brewery's standard lager with additional water added. Light bodied, hint of malt flavor, hops not evident. Brands: Miller Lite (WI), Bud Light (MO).

CONTINENTAL LAGER. Pale to golden in color, with medium maltiness and medium body, some hops in nose. Brands: Heineken (Netherlands), Beck's (Germany), Bacardi Hatuey (MD), Carlsberg Lager (Denmark).

AMBER LAGER. Medium-bodied beer, malty flavor and aroma, sometimes hoppy. Can range in color from deep gold to copper-red. Brands: Abita Amber (LA), Great Lakes Eliot

Ness Lager (OH), Thomas Kemper Amber Lager (WA), Stroh Augsburger Red (MN).

**GERMAN OR BOHEMIAN PILSNER.** Light to medium body, hoppy nose, crisp, hoppy taste. Color ranges from straw to light amber. Rich head. Brands: Pilsner Urquell (Czech Republic), Dock Street Bohemian Pilsner (PA), Lowenbräu Premium Pils (WI), Baderbrau Pilsener (IL).

**DUNKEL (ALSO CALLED DARK LAGER).** Medium- to dark-brown beer with medium hoppiness, medium maltiness, often a roasted or chocolate flavor. Low hoppiness, medium maltiness in aroma. Brands: Beck's Dark (Germany), Stroh Augsburger Dark (MN), Thomas Kemper Bohemian Dunkel (WA), Dixie Blackened Voodoo (LA).

**VIENNA-STYLE LAGER.** Amber to reddish-brown in color; soft maltiness offset by low to medium bitterness. Light to medium in body. Brands: Dos Equis Amber (Mexico), Blue Ridge Amber Lager (MD), Irons American Iron (CO).

**OKTOBERFEST/MÄRZEN.** Two names for the same style of beer. Gold to reddish-brown, very malty, with low to medium bitterness, malty nose. Brands: Berghoff Oktoberfest (WI), Dominion Octoberfest (VA), Hacker-Pschorr Märzen (Germany), Paulaner Oktoberfest Märzen Amber (Germany).

**BOCK.** Traditionally malty and sweet, copper to brown in color, medium- to full-bodied, with a malty nose and just enough hops to balance the malt taste. Brands: New Glarus Uff-da Bock (WI), Schell Bock (MN), Spaten Bock (Germany), Frankenmuth Bock (MI).

**DOPPELBOCK.** A strong bock, medium to dark brown and very sweet. Brands: Schell Doppelbock (MN), Spaten Optimator (Germany), Old Dominion Doppelbock (VA), Paulaner Salvator (Germany).

## SPECIALTY BEERS

Even the world's largest brewers have experimented with adding flavorings beyond malt and hops to their beers. The most popular flavored beers are fruit beers, which can be lagers or ales, but the possibilities are almost endless.

**FRUIT BEERS.** The range of fruit beers is extensive. Brewers make beer out of apples, apricots, blueberries, cherries, raspberries, pineapple, and even passion fruit. Many brewpubs and microbrewers produce fruit beers by taking a basic golden or wheat ale recipe and adding fruit or fruit extract. Belgian brewers add fruit to lambic beer and produce winelike beers such as Lindeman's Kriek, made with cherries, and Liefmans Framboise, made with raspberries. Brands: Celis Raspberry (TX), Pyramid Apricot Ale (WA), Niagara Falls Apple Ale (Canada), Samuel Adams Cherry Wheat (MA).

**OTHER FLAVORED BEERS.** You can find beers flavored with honey (Leinekugel's Honey Weiss, WI), maple syrup (Niagara Falls Maple Wheat, Canada), pumpkin (Buffalo Bill's Pumpkin Ale, CA), green chili (Rogue Mexicali Ale, OR, and Cave Creek Chili Beer, AZ), chocolate (Dixie White Moose, LA), and much more. The incorporation of smoked malt produces smoky-flavored beer, such as Alaskan Smoked Porter (AK), Rogue Smoke (OR), and Aecht Schlenkerla Rauchbier (Germany).

**HOLIDAY BEERS.** During the holiday season, many breweries produce flavored "Christmas beers." These can be either ales or lagers and may be made with cinnamon, nutmeg, fruit, cloves, and various other ingredients. Brands: Anchor's Our Christmas Ale (CA), Berghoff Hazelnut Winter Fest Ale (WI), Pete's Wicked Winter Brew (CA). Other beers produced for the holiday season are simply maltier, hoppier, stronger versions of traditionally styled beers, or are old ales. Brands: Samuel Adams Winter Lager (MA), Sierra Nevada Celebration Ale (CA), Geary's Hampshire Special Ale (ME), Wild Goose Snow Goose Ale (MD).

# INDEX

**A**le(s)
Amber Ale BBQ Sauce, 79
described, 3
Harvest Amber Ale BBQ
Shrimp, 78–79
serving, 6
Ale, stout. **See** Stout
Aloha Ale Sauce, 122
Aloha Ale Sauce, Steak with, 122
Amber ale
BBQ Sauce, 79
Harvest Amber Ale BBQ
Shrimp, 78–79
Amber Ale BBQ Sauce, 79
Anasazi Chicken, 98–99
Ancho Broth, 102
Ancho Butter, 88
Ancho Butter, Spicy Beer-Steamed
Mussels with, 86–88
Appetizers and side dishes
Asiago Cheese Dip with Beer
Bread, 20–21
Bay Shrimp Pestodillas, 12–13
Beer Cheese Spread, 18
Black Bean Dip, 22
Crab and Artichoke Dip, 19
introduction to, 9
Mushroom Pâté, 14–15
Smoked Chicken Nachos with
Beer Cheese Sauce, 10–11
Vegetarian Strudel, 16–17
Artichoke Dip, Crab and, 19
Asiago Cheese Dip with Beer
Bread, 20–21

**B**aby Back Ribs with Stoddard's
Brew BBQ Sauce, 120–21
Badlands Pork Tenderloin, 107
Barley wine, serving, 6
Batter, Beer, 75
Bavarian Pot Roast with Stout
Gravy, 112–13
Bay Shrimp Pestodillas, 12–13
Bean Dip, Black, 22
Bean Sauce, Black, 85
Beef
Bavarian Pot Roast with Stout
Gravy, 112–13
Black-and-Blue Burger, 31
with Black Radish Beer, 114–15
Buffalo or Beef Brisket, 118–19
Steak with Aloha Ale Sauce, 122
Beef with Black Radish Beer,
114–15
Beer
basics of, 2–3
brewpubs and beer cuisine, 1–2, 8
food, matching with, 3–6
kinds of, 3

serving, 6–7
styles, described, 141–49
Beer and Cheese Soup, 48–49
Beer Batter, 75
Beer-Braised Sauerkraut, 33
Beer Bread, 21
Beer Bread, Asiago Cheese Dip
with, 20–21
Beer Broth, Spicy, 87
Beer Cheese Sauce, 10
Beer Cheese Sauce, Smoked
Chicken Nachos with, 10–11
Beer Cheese Spread, 18
Belgian-style ales, serving, 6
Black-and-Blue Burger, 31
Black Bean Dip, 22
Black Bean Sauce, 85
Black Radish Beer, Beef with,
114–15
Black Stout Pecan Pie with Oatmeal
Stout Ice Cream, 136–37
Braised Chicken in Weizen Ale,
92–93
Braised Halibut with Vegetables and
Herbs, 76–77
Bread
Asiago Cheese Dip with Beer,
20–21
Beer, 21
Caesar Salad with Focaccia,
62–63
Focaccia, 63
Brewhouse Chicken Alfredo, 91
Brewpubs, beer cuisine and, 1–2, 8
Buffalo or Beef Brisket, 118–19
Butter, Ancho, 88

**C**abbage
Beer-Braised Sauerkraut, 33
Coleslaw, 121
Caesar Salad with Focaccia, 62–63
Cake, Lemon-Orange Pudding,
128–29
Calzone, Chocolate, 126–27
Caramel Sauce, 139
Caribbean Mango Tuna, 84–85
Cascade Pumpkin BrulÇe, 134–35
Cheese
Asiago Cheese Dip, 20–21
Asiago Cheese Dip with Beer
Bread, 20–21
Beer and Cheese Soup, 48–49
Beer Cheese Sauce, 10
Beer Cheese Spread, 18
Grilled Black Forest Ham and
Gruyère Sandwich, 30
Smoked Chicken Nachos with
Beer Cheese Sauce, 10–11
Cheesecake, Stout, 132–33

Chicken
    Anasazi, 98–99
    Braised Chicken in Weizen
        Ale, 92–93
    Brewhouse Chicken Alfredo, 91
    Cock-A-Leekie Pie, 96–97
    Bayou Sandwich, 28–29
    Cordon Bleu Pizza, 38–40
    Deep Enders, 90
    Grilled Chicken and Sweet Corn
        Risotto, 102–3
    Grilled Chicken Sub, 26–27
    introduction to, 89
    Jalfrajie, 104
    Orange-Cilantro Roasted,
        100–101
    Santa Fe, 94–95
    Smoked Chicken Nachos with
        Beer Cheese Sauce, 10–11
Chicken Bayou Sandwich, 28–29
Chicken Cordon Bleu Pizza, 38–40
Chicken Jalfrajie, 104
Chili, Iron Horse Stout, 52–53
Chili Sauce, Parsilla, 101
Chili Stew, Vegetarian Green, 54–55
Chipotle Sauce, 95
Chocolate Calzone, 126–27
Chocolate Stout Torte, 130–31
Chocolate Truffles, 124
Cilantro Roasted Chicken, Orange-,
    100–101
Cock-A-Leekie Pie, 96–97
Coleslaw, 121
Corn
    Crab and Corn Chowder, 42–43
    Grilled Chicken and Sweet Corn
        Risotto, 102–3
    Grilled Tuna Salad with Corn
        Relish and Peach Salsa, 66–67
    Relish, 67
    Sweet Corn Risotto, 102–3
Corn Relish, 67
Corn Relish and Peach Salsa,
    Grilled Tuna Salad with, 66–67
Crab and Artichoke Dip, 19
Crab and Corn Chowder, 42–43
Creole Sauce, Jambalaya with,
    56–57

Deep Enders Chicken, 90
Desserts
    Black Stout Pecan Pie with
        Oatmeal Stout Ice Cream,
        136–37
    Cascade Pumpkin Brûlée,
        134–35
    Chocolate Calzone, 126–27
    Chocolate Stout Torte, 130–31
    Chocolate Truffles, 124
    Double Triple, The, 125
    introduction to, 123
    Lemon-Orange Pudding Cake,
        128–29
    Stout Cheesecake, 132–33
    Toffee Pudding, 138–40
Dip
    Asiago Cheese, 20–21
    Black Bean, 22

Crab and Artichoke, 19
Dock Street Beer Seafood Fest,
    80–81
Double Triple, The, 125
Düsseldorf Cream Sauce, Pork
    Rouladen with, 108–9

Fettuccine with Weissbier, 61
Fish. See Seafood
Fish and Chips, 75
Flour and Spice Mix, 97
Fluke Pizza, The, 36–37
Focaccia, 63
Focaccia, Caesar Salad with, 62–63

Garlic Paste, Roasted, 39
Garnishes. See Sauces and
    Garnishes
Ginger Vinaigrette, Sesame-, 65
Grilled Black Forest Ham and
    Gruyére Sandwich, 30
Grilled Chicken and Sweet Corn
    Risotto, 102–3
Grilled Chicken Sub, 26–27
Grilled Tuna Salad with Corn Relish
    and Peach Salsa, 66–67
Grilled Vegetable Salad with
    Sesame-Ginger Vinaigrette,
    64–65

Halibut with Vegetables and Herbs,
    Braised, 76–77
Ham and Gruyère Sandwich, Grilled
    Black Forest, 30
Hamburger, Black-and-Blue, 31
Harvest Amber Ale BBQ Shrimp,
    78–79
Herbs, Braised Halibut with
    Vegetables and, 76–77
Homemade Whipped Cream, 140

Ice Cream, Oatmeal Stout, 137
Iron Horse Stout Chili, 52–53
Italian Meat Balls, 106
Italian Tortellini Soup, 46–47

Jambalaya with Creole Sauce,
    56–57

Kennebunkport's Best Reuben,
    32–33

Lager(s)
    described, 3
    serving, 7
Lemon-Orange Pudding Cake,
    128–29
Linguine Oasis, 60

Mango and Papaya Salsa, 85
Mango Tuna, Caribbean, 84–85
Marinade, 100
Marmalade, Red Onion–Sage, 30
Meat. See also specific types
    Baby Back Ribs with Stoddard's
        Brew BBQ Sauce, 120–21
    introduction to, 105
    Italian Meat Balls, 106

Shepherd's Pie, 110–11
Mushroom Pate, 14–15
Mussels with Ancho Butter, Spicy
    Beer-Steamed, 86–88

Nachos with Beer Cheese Sauce,
    Smoked Chicken, 10–11

Oatmeal Stout Ice Cream, 137
Oatmeal Stout Ice Cream, Black
    Stout Pecan Pie with, 136–37
Onion–Sage Marmalade, Red, 30
Onion Soup, Seven, 50–51
Orange-Cilantro Roasted Chicken,
    100–101
Orange Pudding Cake, Lemon-,
    128–29

Papaya Salsa, Mango and, 85
Parsilla Chili Sauce, 101
Pasta
    Fettuccine with Weissbier, 61
    introduction to, 59
    Italian Tortellini Soup, 46–47
    Linguine Oasis, 60
    Penne Pasta, 70–71
    "Sonoma" Shrimp with
        Capellini Pasta, 68–69
    Spicy Angel Hair Pasta, 72
Pate Mushroom, 14–15
Peach Salsa, 66
Peach Salsa, Grilled Tuna Salad
    with Corn Relish and, 66–67
Pecan Pie, Black Stout, 136
Pecan Pie with Oatmeal Stout Ice
    Cream, Black Stout, 136–37
Penne Pasta, 70–71
Pestodillas, Bay Shrimp, 12–13
Pie, Black Stout Pecan, 136
Pita, Veggie, 24–25
Pizza
    Acapulco, 34–35
    Chicken Cordon Bleu, 38–40
    Dough, 40, 127
    Fluke, The, 36–37
    introduction to, 23
Pizza Acapulco, 34–35
Pizza Dough (for Chicken Cordon
    Bleu Pizza), 40
Pizza Dough (for Chocolate
    Calzone), 127
Pork
    Badlands Pork Tenderloin, 107
    Rouladen with Düsseldorf
        Cream Sauce, 108–9
    Spiessbraten, 116–17
Pork Rouladen with Düsseldorf
    Cream Sauce, 108–9
Potatoes
    Fish and Chips, 75
    Wheat Beer Potato Soup, 58
Pot Roast with Stout Gravy,
    Bavarian, 112–13
Poultry. See Chicken
Pudding, Toffee, 138–40
Pudding Cake, Lemon-Orange, 1
    28–29
Pumpkin Brûlée, Cascade, 134–35

Pumpkin-Spiced Salmon, 82–83

Red Onion–Sage Marmalade, 30
Relish
    Corn, 67
    Grilled Tuna Salad with Corn
        Relish and Peach Salsa,
        66–67
Reuben, Kennebunkport's Best,
    32–33
Ribs with Stoddard's Brew BBQ
    Sauce, Baby Back, 120–21
Risotto, Grilled Chicken and Sweet
    Corn, 102–3
Risotto, Sweet Corn, 102–3
Roasted Garlic Paste, 39

Sage Marmalade, Red Onion–, 30
Salads
    Caesar Salad with Focaccia,
        62–63
    Grilled Tuna Salad with Corn
        Relish and Peach Salsa,
        66–67
    Grilled Vegetable Salad with
        Sesame-Ginger Vinaigrette,
        64–65
    introduction to, 59
Salmon, Pumpkin-Spiced, 82–83
Salmon Chowder, Smoked, 44–45
Salsa
    Mango and Papaya, 85
    Peach, 66
Sandwich(es)
    Black-and-Blue Burger, 31
    Chicken Cordon Bayou, 28–29
    Grilled Black Forest Ham and
        Gruyère, 30
    Grilled Chicken Sub, 26–27
    introduction to, 23
    Kennebunkport's Best Reuben,
        32–33
    Veggie Pita, 24–25
Santa Fe Chicken, 94–95
Sauces and Garnishes
    Aloha Ale Sauce, 122
    Amber Ale BBQ Sauce, 79
    Beer Cheese Sauce, 10
    Black Bean Sauce, 85
    Caramel Sauce, 139
    Chipotle Sauce, 95
    Corn Relish, 67
    Creole Sauce, 57
    Düsseldorf Cream Sauce, 109
    Mango and Papaya Salsa, 85
    Marinade, 100
    Parsilla Chili Sauce, 101
    Peach Salsa, 66
    Red Onion–Sage Marmalade, 30
    Roasted Garlic Paste, 39
    Spicy Beer Broth, 87
    Stoddard's Brew BBQ Sauce,
        120
Sauerkraut, Beer-Braised, 33
Seafood
    Bay Shrimp Pestodillas, 12–13
    Braised Halibut with Vegetables
        and Herbs, 76–77

Caribbean Mango Tuna, 84–85
Crab and Artichoke Dip, 19
Crab and Corn Chowder, 42–43
Dock Street Beer Seafood Fest,
    80–81
Fish and Chips, 75
Grilled Tuna Salad with Corn
    Relish and Peach Salsa,
    66–67
Harvest Amber Ale BBQ
    Shrimp, 78–79
introduction to, 73
Pumpkin-Spiced Salmon, 82–83
Smoked Salmon Chowder,
    44–45
"Sonoma" Shrimp with
    Capellini Pasta, 68–69
Spicy Beer Shrimp, 74
Spicy Beer-Steamed Mussels
    with Ancho Butter, 86–88
Sesame-Ginger Vinaigrette, Grilled
    Vegetable Salad with, 64–65
Seven Onion Soup, 50–51
Shepherd's Pie, 110–11
Shrimp
    Bay Shrimp Pestodillas, 12–13
    Harvest Amber Ale BBQ, 78–79
    "Sonoma" Shrimp with
        Capellini Pasta, 68–69
    Spicy Beer, 74
Side dishes. See Appetizers and side
    dishes
Smoked Chicken Nachos with Beer
    Cheese Sauce, 10–11
Smoked Salmon Chowder, 44–45
"Sonoma" Shrimp with Capellini
    Pasta, 68–69
Soup(s). See also Stew(s)
    Beer and Cheese, 48–49
    Crab and Corn Chowder, 42–43
    introduction to, 41
    Italian Tortellini, 46–47
    Seven Onion, 50–51
    Smoked Salmon Chowder,
        44–45
    Wheat Beer Potato, 58
Spice Mix, Flour and, 97
Spicy Angel Hair Pasta, 72
Spicy Beer Broth, 87
Spicy Beer Shrimp, 74
Spicy Beer-Steamed Mussels with
    Ancho Butter, 86–88
Spiessbraten, 116–17
Spread, Beer Cheese, 18
Steak with Aloha Ale Sauce, 122
Stew(s). See also Soup(s)
    introduction to, 41
    Iron Horse Stout Chili, 52–53
    Jambalaya with Creole Sauce,
        56–57
    Vegetarian Green Chili, 54–55
Stoddard's Brew BBQ Sauce, Baby
    Back Ribs with, 120–21
Stout
    Bavarian Pot Roast with Stout
        Gravy, 112–13
    Black Stout Pecan Pie with
        Oatmeal Stout Ice Cream,

136–37
    Cheesecake, 132–33
    Chocolate Stout Torte, 130–31
    Iron Horse Stout Chili, 52–53
    serving, 6
Stout Cheesecake, 132–33
Strudel, Vegetarian, 16–17
Sub, Grilled Chicken, 26–27
Sweet Corn Risotto, 102–3

Toffee Pudding, 138–40
Torte, Chocolate Stout, 130–31
Tortellini Soup, Italian, 46–47
Truffles, Chocolate, 124
Tuna, Caribbean Mango, 84–85
Tuna Salad with Corn Relish and
    Peach Salsa, Grilled, 66–67

Vegetables/vegetarian. See also
        specific vegetables
    Braised Halibut with Vegetables
        and Herbs, 76–77
    Green Chili Stew, 54–55
    Grilled Vegetable Salad with
        Sesame-Ginger Vinaigrette,
        64–65
    Pita, 24–25
    Strudel, 16–17
Vegetarian Green Chili Stew, 54–55
Vegetarian Strudel, 16–17
Veggie Pita, 24–25
Vinaigrette, Grilled Vegetable Salad
    with Sesame-Ginger, 64–65

Weissbier (weizenbier)
    Fettuccine with, 61
Weizen Ale, Braised Chicken in,
    92–93
Wheat beer(s)
    Potato Soup, 58
    serving, 7
Wheat Beer Potato Soup, 58
Whipped Cream, Homemade, 140

# STATE-BY-STATE
# INDEX OF BREWPUBS

## ALABAMA
Magic City Brewery, 420 21st St., Birmingham, AL 35233, 205-328-2739

Montgomery Brewing Co., 12 W. Jefferson St., Montgomery, AL 36104, 334-834-2739

## ARIZONA
Hops! Bistro & Brewery, 7000 E. Camelback, Scottsdale, AZ 85251, 602-945-4677

Prescott Brewing Co., 130 W. Gurley St., Suite A , Prescott, AZ 86301, 520-771-2795

## ARKANSAS
Ozark Brewing Co., 430 W. Dickson St., Fayetteville, AR 72701, 501-521-2739

Vino's Brewpub, 923 W. Seventh, Little Rock, AR 72201, 501-375-8466

## CALIFORNIA
Barley & Hopps Brewery, 201 S. B St., San Mateo, CA 94401, 415-348-7808

Buckhorn Saloon at Anderson Valley Brewing Co., 14081 State Highway 128, Boonville, CA 95415, 707-895-2337

Dempsey's Ale House at Sonoma Brewing Co., 50 E. Washington St., Petaluma, CA 94952, 707-765-9694

Marin Brewing Co., 1809 Larkspur Landing, Larkspur, CA 94939, 415-461-4677

North Coast Brewing Co., 455 N. Main St., Fort Bragg, CA 95437, 707-964-2739

Stoddard's Brewhouse & Eatery, 111 S. Murphy Ave., Sunnyvale, CA 94086, 408-733-7824

Sudwerk Privatbrauerei Hübsch, 2001 Second St., Davis, CA 95616, 916-756-2739

## COLORADO
Il Vicino Wood Oven, Pizza & Brewery, 136 E. Second St., Salida, CO 81201, 719-539-5219.

Walnut Brewery, 1123 Walnut St., Boulder, CO 80302, 303-447-1345

Wynkoop Brewing Co., 1634 18th St., Denver, CO 80202. 303-297-2700

## FLORIDA
Ragtime Tavern & Grill, 207 Atlantic Blvd., Atlantic Beach, FL 32233, 904-241-7877

## GEORGIA
Phoenix Brewing Co., 5600 Roswell Road, Suite 21, Atlanta, GA 30342, 404-843-2739

## HAWAII
Gordon Biersch, 101 Ala Moana Blvd., Honolulu, HI 96813, 808-599-4877

## IDAHO
TableRock Brewpub & Grill, 705 Fulton St., Boise, ID 83702, 208-342-0944

## ILLINOIS
Flatlander's Chophouse and Brewery, 200 Village Green, Lincolnshire, IL 60069, 847-821-1234

Goose Island Brewing Co., 1800 N. Clybourn, Chicago, IL 60614, 312-915-0071

Mickey Finn's Brewery, 412 N. Milwaukee Ave., Libertyville, IL 60048, 847-362-6688

Mill Rose Brewing Co., 45 South Barrington Road
South Barrington, IL 6001, 847-382-7691

## INDIANA

Broad Ripple Brewpub, 842 E. 65th St., Indianapolis, IN 46220,
317-253-2739

## KENTUCKY

Bluegrass Brewing Co., 3929 Shelbyville Road, Louisville, KY 40207,
502-899-7070

## MAINE

Federal Jack's Restaurant & Brewpub, 8 Western Ave.,
Kennebunk, ME 04043, 207-967-4311

Gritty McDuff's Brew Pub, 396 Fore St., Portland, ME 04101,
207-772-2739

## MARYLAND

Olde Towne Tavern & Brewing Co., 227 E. Diamond Ave.,
Gaithersburg, MD 20877, 301-948-4200

The Wharf Rat Camden Yards, 206 W. Pratt St., Baltimore MD 21201,
410-244-8900

## MASSACHUSETTES

Boston Beer Works, 61 Brookline Ave.,Boston, MA 02215, 617-536-2337

Commonwealth Brewing Co., 138 Portland St., Boston, MA 02114,
617-523-8383

## MICHIGAN

Grizzly Peak Brewing Co., 120 W. Washington, Ann Arbor, MI 48104,
313-741-7325

## MINNESOTA

Mill Street Brewing Co., 57 S. Hamline Ave., St. Paul, MN 55105,
612-690-1946

## MISSOURI

75th Street Brewery, 520 W. 75th St.,Kansas City, MO 64114, 816-523-4677

Ebbets Field, 1027 E. Walnut, Springfield, MO 65806, 417-865-5050

St. Louis Brewery and Tap Room, 2100 Locust St., St. Louis, MO 63102,
314-241-2337

## NEBRASKA

Crane River Brewpub & Cafe, 200 N. 11th St., Lincoln, NE 68508,
402-476-7766

Jaipur Restaurant and Brewing Co., 10922 Elm St. Omaha, NE 68144,
402-392-7331

## NEW HAMPSHIRE

Elm City Brewing Co., Colony Mill Marketplace, Keene, NH 03431,
603-355-3335

Italian Oasis & Brewery, 106 Main St., Littleton, NH 03561, 603-444-6995

## NEW JERSEY

Triumph Brewing Co., 138 Nassau St., Princeton, NJ, 609-924-7855

## NEW MEXICO

Eske's Brew Pub & Eatery, 106 DeGeorges Lane, Taos, NM 87571,
505-758-1517

## NEW YORK

Empire Brewing Co.,120 Walton St., Syracuse, NY 13202, 315-475-2337

Gentleman Jim's Bistro-Brewery, 522 Dutchess Turnpike,
Poughkeepsie, NY 12603, 914-485-5467

Hyde Park Brewing Co., 514 Albany Post Road, Hyde Park, NY 12538,
914-229-8277

Zip City Brewing Co., 3 W. 18th St., New York, NY 10011, 212-366-6333

## NORTH CAROLINA

Cottonwood Grille & Brewery, 122 Blowing Rock Road, Boone, NC 28607,
704-264-7111

Weeping Radish Brewery, Highway 64, Manteo, NC 27954, 919-473-1157

## NORTH DAKOTA
Great Northern Restaurant & Brewery, 425 Broadway, Fargo, ND 58102, 701-235-9707

Rattlesnake Creek Brewery and Grill, 2 W. Villard, Dickinson, ND 58602, 701-225-9518

## OKLAHOMA
Pete's Place, 120 S.W. Eighth St, Krebs, OK 74554, 918-423-2042

## OREGON
The Black Rabbit Restaurant at Edgefield Manor, 2126 S.W. Halsey St., Troutdale, OR 97060,503-492-4686

## PENNSYLVANIA
Dock Street Brewing Co., 2 Logan Square, Philadelphia, PA 19103, 215-496-0413

The Black Angus at Stoudt Brewery, State Route 272, Adamstown, PA 19501, 215-484-4387

The Church Brew Works, 3525 Liberty Ave., Pittsburgh, PA 15201, 412-688-8200

## RHODE ISLAND
Union Station Brewing Co., 36 Exchange Terrace, Providence, RI 02903, 401-274-2739

## SOUTH CAROLINA
Hunter-Gatherer Brewery, 900 Main St., Columbia, SC 29201, 803-748-0540

## SOUTH DAKOTA
Firehouse Brewing Co., 610 Main St., Rapid City, SD 57701, 605-348-1915

## TENNESSEE
Big River Grille and Brewing Works, 222 Broad St., Chattanooga, TN 37400, 423-267-2739

## TEXAS
Coppertank Brewing Co., 504 Trinity St., Austin, TX 78701, 512-478-8444

## UTAH
Eddie McStiff's Restaurant and Micro Brewery, 57 S. Main St., Moab, UT 84532, 801-259-2337

Fuggles Microbrewery, 367 W. 200 South, Salt Lake City, UT 84101, 801-363-7000

## VERMONT
The Vermont Pub & Brewery, 144 College St., Burlington, VT 05401, 802-865-0500

## VIRGINIA
Richbrau Brewing Co. and Restaurant, 1214 E. Cary St., Richmond, VA 23219, 804-644-3018

## WASHINGTON
Leavenworth Brewery, 636 Front St., Leavenworth, WA 98826, 509-548-4545

Pyramid Alehouse & Thomas Kemper Brewery, 91 S. Royal Brougham Way, Seattle, WA 98134, 206-682-8322

## WASHINGTON D.C.
Capitol City Brewing Co., 2 Massachusetts Ave., Washington, DC 20002, 202-842-2337

## WISCONSIN
Brewmasters Pub, Restaurant, & Brewery, 4017 80th St., Kenosha, WI 53142, 414-694-9050

Randy's FunHunters Brewery, 841 E. Milwaukee St., Whitewater, WI 53190, 414-473-8000